PAGES
PENNED
IN
PANDEMIC

A COLLECTIVE

EDITED BY KAYLA KING & JUSTIN MAHER

Masthead
Kayla King, Founder, Editor-in-Chief, and Publisher
Justin Maher, Co-Founder and Editor
Cover art by Kayla King
Book design by Kayla King

Paperback ISBN: 9798554964589

TABLE OF CONTENTS

TABLE OF CONTENTS

TABLE OF CONTENTS

TABLE OF CONTENTS

TABLE OF CONTENTS

LETTERS FROM THE EDITORS

When I called my best friend on September 23, 2020 to pitch what felt like an impossible idea, to collect pages penned in pandemic, I could not fathom what this project would become.

Throughout October, November, and December, this book kept us connected despite the many miles and cities between us. In time, however, I know the collective will transform, serving as a means to connect future readers to our past selves.

Perhaps you have just plucked this book off the shelf for the first time. Maybe it's been ten years since and you only talk about 2020 as the *lost year*. Whenever you find these words, I hope you will look at this collective as a mosaic. Lovely, right? To take the shattered pieces of a tumultuous year and reassemble them into something beautiful?

I must admit, I was not the first to call this collective a mosaic, but rather the explanation resonated with me long after it was spoken by someone most dear. I held these pieces in a stack of tangible pages, feeling grateful and inspired and at times heartbroken over this collective.

Whether writing about grief or fear, loss or new life, lovers or brothers or dogs, there is a sense of connectedness woven throughout every work, which begged us to piece together this book with care.

If you're reading this now, it means the book no longer belongs to us, the editors. But then again, I don't think it ever really belonged to us. Stories are meant to be shared.

- Kayla King, Founder and Editor-in-Chief

LETTERS FROM THE EDITORS

Hello Readers,

First off, thank you for buying this book. It should be known that what you hold in your hands would not exist without Kayla King. Energizer Bunny, that one. Thanks Kayla!

One the largest draws to develop this project, other than sharing an editorial by-line with my best friend, was learning that all of our proceeds from the printed edition will be going off to assist *826National*, a nonprofit organization committed to awakening and embracing the power of writing in education. Some may have heard it said that there are no new stories out there, that they've all been told, or everything is a remake. Well, I disagree. This collective insists that as long as there are new voices writing, we will find new life in stories to tell.

In addition to being an amazing opportunity to indulge in the pleasure of hands-on editing, this experience also brought new words to learn, which reminded me how we poets and authors can not only entertain and inspire others, but also enlighten and educate one another. Combing through these pages, I expanded my vocabulary by at least sixteen words (sojourn, pemmican, flotsam, flaneuse, to name a few). Enough to level-up my Scrabble game, I'd say. So, thanks for that, writers!

In the first week of submissions, we were treated to Meghan Malachi's "21 Years." It became clear that we were going to be met with some deeply talented voices in this collection. Even after two months, over 340 submissions, and seemingly countless pages, we came upon the final submission to read: "[untitled]" by Wim Owe. I was enthralled, and am still in love with that final line, "I promise I won't revise this until I am no longer myself." Snaps shot from my fingers rapid enough to spark fire or blister my thumb.

To those who participated in this collection with either your voice or your time, thank you! To those who are reading this, thank you again! Please enjoy and spread these words. I am immensely proud of this collective effort, of all those involved, and what we made together. Be proud. Be well.

- Justin Maher, Co-Founder and Editor

P.S.
To Kayla King:
Thank you for bringing me on board for this,
for reigniting my creativity. I'm so glad to be inked into these pages with you.
Thank you for your mind. You impress me. Every. Day.
And I love you.

DAY 49

SHER TING

The sky burst into flames and my mind
twisted itself into knots, parsing sunlight
from an orphaned reflection

Time flowed backwards, staggering through the stale
buttered air, its cave-mouth lusting for the nectar of
sweet-briar and the dew of meadow grass beyond the
splintering walls

The sun had bowed out from the sky as I muscled crop circles
from ink and ivory sheets, trying and trying in vain to ignite
a flame upon my mind's wick, and
in the after-hour, I ribbed a sinew
of river through the fragmented loam of reality

Sometimes, silence was an echo of a memory,
incubating muted reminisces of glazed waters and open skies.

Other times, silence achieved
a corporeal form, sitting at the corner of the room,
an eye to me—
an eye to the other side

Today, silence was my breath growing ever larger
till it enveloped the room, leaving little space for my thoughts.

My thoughts became so small
I threaded them through the eye of a dream.

NAVIGATING NEW WORLDS

JASON DE KOFF

In the middle of the night,
I awake at the top,
of a giant roller coaster,
at that point when,
you can't be lifted higher,
and before you start,
to plummet.

When you realize,
there is no going back,
no escape,
but the inevitable,
sinking feeling,
jumble of organs,
breathless torture,
unknown fear,
cascading,
through every neuron,
in lickety-split,
fast time marches.

But there is no drop,
because I remain poised,
a cat negotiating the fencetop,
with every possible scenario,
a motion picture,
with alternating play/pause features.

Until the light outside,
pierces my eyelids,
ends this waking dream,
and once more I lift,
buckler and breastplate,

and with their familiar weight,
upon my hardened limbs,
I face the plunge.

IN RETROGRADE

SK GROUT

I am not leaping, not quavering
but lying flat—watching the sky
change its relationship to bitter black.

Without the moon, a long gown
white sleeks into the night. A singing?
A bird? A memory of freedom?

The dancing dream increases volume
once the wind takes hold.

A double bass plays through the evening,
timbre almost impenetrable to sense.
It waits, too, between notes,
the space hanging like a bridge:

I am night-thinking, not day-dreaming.

Clouds string the air with post-revelation.
I turn and toss, never sleep
alter my relationship to black bitter.
A bird? A memory of freedom? A singing?

The indigo rustle of a sky backwards,
splintered, unloved stars, the dawn
chorus sweetness scarfing time.
Night's logic wends the path
and I gain insomnia's knowledge.

[UNTITLED]

WIM OWE

Moon, all the years
to be eaten lightly
rather than stay held
weight, worn smooth
and wind. Shifting
rocks in the sun
taught me to dream
be lost in wanting
my fire choked out
as the sun cooks
that pile up beneath
to me, Moon, to winch
our breathing room
the ghost we'll become.

up there, the rattle
on the floor. We don't
or how we find
but we want out,
other place we can see
has stung the gaps
and sanitized the scars
to sleep, but why
as I'm being dragged
the weight of my brain?

apart have driven me
in your jagged crags
down by our world's
by the shock of waves
light and stifling noise,
and sleep in shadows
on paper so I wouldn't
to be swept away,
on this hurtling rock
these shards of glass
my feet. Better to come
yourself down into
wearing the face of

I can hear screaming
of plastic cups
know how they got there
ourselves among them,
and your face is the only
to believe. The rum
between my teeth
of the day so I'm ready
can't I see your face
behind my eyes by

I promise I won't revise this
until I am no longer myself.

PARTICLES

GRACE ALICE EVANS

the barriers

       are lingering

           deep

      in their repose

i remain in the courtyard

of their yellowing grasp

            a dulling gust

sweeps me into the

          corners

      and crevices

of existence

      i oscillate

        half-way

benumbed and intense states

a continuous headache,   recoiling

in fear of the feral sunlight

        straining from the vacant window

i recognize each faint change in the stillness of the air

each morning devoted to snatching at the

          particles of legitimacy

     scattered

in-between dreams and night-visions.

TRANSITION

JENNY MAVEETY

When the sun finally rose, I was in the garden. The night had been cool and calm, but once light started to peek from behind the tree line, the wind picked up. I sat among the onion and carrot tops. They moved in the wind, sheltered by the large stalks of tomato and sweet corn that towered over them. I looked across the garden and to the field beyond. The barley grass swayed in great waves.

I turned to the house behind me. The white shutters were open, pinned against the light blue siding that began to chip this winter. Small finger streaks marked the inside of the bedroom windows in smudgy lines. The porch swing was almost completely still, and I felt the urge to sit.

My body started to move but settled itself into the dirt again.

I didn't want to move, really.

I wanted to be here.

I scooted forward until my fingertips met the petals of the purple coneflowers and black-eyed Susan's and pink asters that lined the edges of the garden. There were marigolds down below, for the pests, but they reminded me of the past, of years where marigolds sprinkled the flower baskets and wilted away when the cold winds of autumn came.

Here in the garden, I took large gulps of morning air. I wanted to fill every cell in my body with new oxygen. I wanted to be remade of something bright and unblemished. There was always something special about the air in the morning.

The sun crept over the treetops and touched my face. I closed my eyes. I felt the warmth and was met with the realization of the power, the sheer force that is the sun. No matter what happened to me, to us, to the little bugs and onion greens, the sun would be there as a silent and unbiased observer.

People were fragile and penetrable just like every other living thing.

But I thought I would like to be the sun. Far away and indifferent yet burning with life.

I turned back to the house again, but heard no sounds. Part of me traveled deep into the forest. Far off in the distance, a pack of coyotes devoured a fallen deer, a red-headed woodpecker hacked through bark for bugs, and a black bear and her cubs paraded through ferns on thick, furry paws.

Unlike those creatures, I wasn't ready to move. If I left the garden, the reticence that enveloped me so easily here would be abandoned. But the dirt was damp. I tiptoed around where I assumed the plants to be, mud clinging to my bare feet.

As the minutes passed, my skin protested, prickling with heat from the sun. Though the wind died down, I didn't move. Every sensation was another reminder. I was alive. I could feel.

Flecks of red were lodged deep under several of my nails and I picked at them until they came free. I brushed myself off and noticed several specks of the same color splattered lightly on my overalls. I searched deep into my memory to remember when I had painted last, or what berry had left its juices on my clothing, but I couldn't place it.

Late last night as I did the dishes after dinner, I looked out the kitchen windows and admired the hundreds of fireflies playing in the field. Their neon light reflected the bright, whimsical aesthetic I tried to create in our home. Only pale yellow hugged the dusty drywall and I hated it. The dim light only served to showcase the loathsome color and state of the walls and it gave me a headache.

"We need some new light bulbs," I said to Liam.

"Yeah, you always say that."

He sat on the couch, sprawled in all directions, reading yesterday's newspaper. Where was I? Doing all the housework as usual. Keeping track of the girls as they sprinted up and down the staircase and around me over and over and over again.

"Girls, can you settle down please?" I asked. "Mommy's getting a headache."

They yelled louder over me. I scrubbed away at a plate that was mostly clean. I could *feel* the dirt on it, even though I couldn't see it. I forced the sponge down onto the thin porcelain. I pushed harder to

18

cover the noise between my ears that was heavy and biting like a table saw. The zing of their screams forced further and further into my head until the plate finally shattered under my weight and filled the sink with white shards.

Blood leaked slowly from my right thumb and I ran it under cold water. The noise stopped.

This had happened before. Usually it was when I was in one of my periods of transition. That's what I called them. During those times, everything in the world seemed grey and hazy. It was like I could still see what was happening, but I couldn't feel it, I couldn't be close to it. Usually Liam made me stay locked in our bedroom for several days in a row and I detested him for it. I knew it for what it was: I was learning. I was understanding more about the world and my place in it. I could see reality in a different lens, one other people weren't allowed to see through. I was glad for it, even if I couldn't remember most of what happened later.

I took a breath and continued to do the rest of the dishes.

Liam came over and laid his hand on my shoulder. I jumped at his touch.

"You okay?" he asked.

"Fine." I smiled.

He hesitated a moment, then walked back to his place on the couch. The girls had scurried upstairs to their room when the plate broke and I was glad of it. I just wanted some quiet.

I looked out the window again. Even though it was very dark, I could see the faint outline of the thin, wire fence that encircled my garden. I'd put it up myself last year and shortly after, I planted the marigolds. I knew they were peeking through the ground, their bright yellow, orange, and red heads that glowed in the sunshine. It made the garden look happier, I thought, and more full. I wanted to be amongst them now, away from the chaos of this house.

When the dishes were dried and put away, I went upstairs to give the girls a bath. They were wild without sleep and full bellies and I had to hold them each down to get them undressed. Sadie, only three, thought this was hilarious, their shared nakedness, and began laughing hysterically while rolling around on the floor. Meghan had taken baths with Sadie since she was a baby, so I didn't understand what was so different and funny this time.

19

I felt the noise coming on again, that familiar screeching deafness.

"Enough!" I said.

They both stopped. Sadie's lip curled like she was about to cry, and I looked away. I was too tired.

I picked her up and plopped her in the bath as Meghan got in behind her. They looked at me wide-eyed, waiting for something.

"What?" I asked.

Meghan looked away, but tears streaked Sadie's soft, pink cheeks and I left the bathroom. I just needed to relax. I knew if this were another transition, I would be glad for it in the end, even if it was excruciating now. I didn't want anyone to know, either. I was tired of being condemned to my bed like a prisoner.

Liam walked into the bedroom and laid flat on the bed, just like he was on the couch.

"Do you want to give me a hand?" I asked.

"With what?"

"The girls. They're in the bath."

"You're so much better with them than me."

"And don't you want to get better?"

"What?" He sat up.

"Don't you want to at least *try* to do more with them?"

"Where is this coming from?"

I felt my belly boil with rage. Blue sparks filled my nerves and shot out of my skin in all directions. I felt like I was short circuiting.

"Where is this coming from? How about the fact that you do almost *nothing* for me or the kids? I am here every single day and night. You go off for work, for your friends, for whatever it is you do when you're not here, and I'm sure it's quite a lot. When you do decide to be here, you're lounging around the house as if you don't even live here! As if you're a guest! Well, let me tell you something right now—"

"Have you been taking your medication?"

My body went stiff and the heat from my anger dissipated off me instantly. The room became ice cold and I was trapped in its chill.

I couldn't say anything.

"Have you?" he pressed.

I knew he didn't know about me dropping the pills in the field last week. He couldn't have known; he doesn't bother to check on things until they affect him. Even though I knew this, I got the sneaking suspicion that he knew something I didn't. I felt like his eyes were examining me, finding the flaws and faults that I'd tried to hide as the transition came on.

I walked into the bathroom and slammed the door shut.

Liam came and rapped with his fist. I pictured him covered in dirt with worms poking their way around his chest.

"Alice, open the door."

I stared at the nicks before me, the places where wood and paint used to be, when things were perfect. I remembered when it was just me and Liam in our cottage. It was perfect. He was perfect. He used to scoop me out of the car after work and carry me into the house. He made candlelit dinners and we left the windows open. Little moths would sometimes join us, their noiseless wings fluttering around the flickering flames on the table.

Something changed. It was slow, over the course of a few years, but it felt so black and white. One minute there was peace, the next a dark chasm of pain. Nothing would ever be the same again. There was no harmony in this penitentiary we called our life.

I screamed for him to shut up. I screamed it until my throat was raw and no moisture licked my lips.

I was screaming it as he busted into the room and grabbed the girls out of the tub. I stood there, immobile, howling, as he rushed out and locked them all into the girls' room.

When I was done and not another sound could come out of me, I tidied up the bathroom. There was water everywhere. The girls were never thinking of anybody besides themselves. What is it about people, human beings, that make them so selfish? So unaware of others? Of the ones who take care of them day and night, rain or shine, no matter how tired they are, no matter how much they don't want to; what is it that makes them so superior to *me*?

When I'd had my first transition, Liam told me after that it wasn't good. While I came out of the period of change feeling refreshed and more knowledgeable, Liam said I'd tried to hurt Meghan. Sadie wasn't born yet, but she was growing inside me. According to Liam, I'd taken Meghan outside to the barley field and tried to bury her. He found me out there with a spade in one hand while the other was trying to force Meghan's arms to stay still as I piled dirt on top of her. He said I was whispering about Sadie, though not with her name. He said I was calling her "creature" and "parasite."

Every part of that transition is covered in a haze that I can only see through when another transition is coming. After that day, Liam forced me to an inpatient facility where I stayed for nearly two months. That's when I started taking the pills.

Once the bathroom was clean, I went downstairs to see if Liam had left a mess of any of his things. Surprisingly, he hadn't. But, I had a feeling he'd never make a mess of his things again. Same with the girls. They could be a part of the transition.

I decided right then that they would be. They would see what I see, and they would learn. There was no way around this. I had to break the cycle we'd been locked into for so many years.

I walked silently up the stairs, careful to avoid the creaks that were provoked by stepping too hard on stair three, too far to the left on stair six, and right in the middle of the last stair to the top. I walked in the spaces on the wood that were just barely dipped in, just enough to know that the path had been well-worn.

I knew I had to be quiet and gentle to coax them out of the room. I didn't want to scare them, I really didn't. This had to be approached with care, so they would listen. Just for this one time, they would listen to me. I would have the tranquility I once did. I deserved that much.

I stopped at the top of the stairs and peeked through the curtain to look at the garden below. My true joy. The one place I had refuge in every day. Every flower, every vegetable and fruit, every hedge placed meticulously in perfect order. It was mine and I made sure it was flawless.

Sadie whimpered in the girls' room and I heard Liam shushing her. Why hadn't he just taken them and left? If he was so afraid. Would he ever think of something as simple as that?

"Girls, I brought up some ice cream for dessert."

My hoarse voice was met with silence.

"I just want to talk. Liam, open the door please. We need to work this out as a family."

"Get out of here, Alice. You need help."

I knocked on the door and tried the handle. We'd never installed a lock, but I couldn't turn it.

"Take your hand off the doorknob, Liam."

"No. Go. Just go and I will call the doctor in the morning."

"This is my house. Where do you think I'd go? I have something really important to show all of you."

"It doesn't matter. You're scaring the girls."

"Meghan, Sadie, come on out. Mommy just wants to talk to you for a few minutes."

I pictured the three of them huddled together on the floor. Sadie and Meghan's blonde hair all wet and knotted, needing to be brushed, wrapped up in clothing Liam had been too lazy to put on them.

"Did you brush their hair?" I asked.

"What? No. Is that what you're worried about right now?"

"Liam, if you don't brush their hair now, when it's wet, it'll hurt more later when it's dry. Come on girls, let me brush your hair. You don't want all your hair to fall out if I brush it later, do you?"

"Don't talk to them, Alice. You need to leave. We aren't coming out until you leave."

"Fine, I'll go."

I got right up to the crease in the door and whispered to Liam: "You're all going to learn. I will show you the truth."

I felt myself float down the stairs and leave my body on the landing. I was detached from my physical self as I left. Most of me stayed to see what would happen. The rest of me got in the car and sped down the road. I waited, at the end of the driveway.

The part of me that stayed saw Liam slowly open the girls' bedroom door and shut it behind him. The part of me that stayed watched as Liam tucked the girls into bed and went to call the police. The part of me that stayed grinned when Liam realized I'd taken his phone with me and the only car that worked. The part of me that stayed followed Liam and the girls into our bedroom where he locked the door and windows and propped a chair underneath the doorknob, thinking that would be enough protection until the morning. The part of me that stayed, laughed.

With the floodlights turned off, I stood for a while, looking up at the stars so I could see the sky in full. Our closest neighbor was miles away. Nothing would disturb me.

I walked slowly to the house after an hour had passed. I took off my shoes so I could feel the painful crunch of gravel underneath my soles and wonder at the tiny pieces that got lodged between my toes.

The earth was unforgiving, and we had grown so accustomed to comfort and ease. I felt the different parts of myself move and dance until they came together. Being out in the night, I felt like I was finally becoming a part of it all. Like I was finally on the path I was meant to travel. The pieces of me had aligned.

I went in through the storm cellar. I climbed my way up the stairs. Each step counted, deliberate. I was heading for something I'd never had before, and I could taste it. I licked my lips.

I stopped in the kitchen to look for the old, wooden mallet that was kept underneath the sink. I threw half used cleaning bottles and sponges onto the floor behind me. I lifted up the rotting piece of plywood near the back. Liam thought I wouldn't find this hiding spot, but I did years ago. It was my father's mallet, and I could never seem to give it up, even though I had no real use for it. Tonight, I understood why.

I closed the cupboard and examined the state of our house once again. I would never come back to it, so this was my parting farewell. I waved goodbye to the leak in the ceiling near the furthest east-facing window, goodbye to my grandmother's ripped and torn antique chaise lounge, goodbye, finally, to the chipping yellow paint plastered on every wall, which peeled to reveal an even more grotesque yellow underneath.

I inched up to the bedroom door, whispering to myself that it would all be over soon.

* * *

I stood. I stretched my throbbing arms and tried to wipe the red off me once again. I squished my toes in the drying dirt. It felt coarse and hot, such a difference from how it felt in the soft night. The house looked the same. Nothing had moved. The smudges had not been cleaned. Liam must have left because the car wasn't there. He must

24

have taken the girls with him. Good. They deserve a day out of the house. Just like I do.

I looked to the field near the forest with the barley grass. There were three patches in the field that looked pushed in. I wondered why. I caught a glimpse of my spade stuck hard in the earth near the edge of the garden. The handle was covered in brown and the metal coated in a shiny red.

The greyness of the transition was almost gone, but it lingered. I accepted this. The brightness of the morning cleared my headache, and I was more aligned with my peace than ever before.

The bright orange of the sprouting tulips caught my eye before I got up to leave the garden. I crouched again to examine them, to feel them pushing through, pushing, and aching so hard to reach the sun, to just reach that flame which would give them life. Even though they knew nothing of death, of the inevitable extermination they would endure like us all, they reached for the glorious heat like it was all they'd ever need. I, too, reached for the sun.

MEDITATION ON THE HEAT DEATH OF THE UNIVERSE

DAPHNE DAUGHERTY

I. Formation

Tell me how you hide it, how you conceal
the way that a voice can rub against your skin
insinuating itself into the base of your throat
in figure eights, butter-soft and sharp like the
sunset over Joshua Tree National Park, where
they say you can see all the way back to the
Big Bang if you close your eyes, where
the women you love trade dagger blows
in the gathering dark, where the heat on the wind
reminds you of someone you've never met, someone
who could impede the progress of maximum entropy
and keep you whole, keep you from
desiccating in a desert of your own making.

II. Stellification

Tell me how you bear it, how you endure
when a scent filters up from the pillowcase, settles
somewhere between your ribcage and the edge of a knife
where the half-life of longing approaches infinity
and the apparent magnitude of fireflies rivals that
of J043947.08+163415.7 when you're only microns
away, even though his teeth flash in the brilliant dark
echoing the starbirth clouds that tower like scholar's stones
in the Eagle Nebula and you don't remember the first time
you looked up and saw your future in the cosmos
but you do remember this, remember thinking you saw
Polaris in his eyes but found yourself lost anyway, faded
into the background radiation of a universe already too cold for life.

III. Expansion

Tell me how you kill it, how you destroy
the part of you that wants too much but offers nothing, that
fools itself into believing that the potential energy in your chest
can breach an event horizon, can become something
dense and hot and strong enough to capture light, when
everything comes down to an equation in the end
and you've never known enough of the variables to see
into the distant future but you thought you saw enough for tonight, for
tomorrow, for your own centripetal force to overcome
the inertia of a steady state heart, red shifting away from west
to east until it flies away over Lake Michigan and disappears
into a singularity where you cannot follow, only to reappear
somewhere 14 billion light-years away where physics don't apply.

IV. Extinction

Tell me nothing. Keep your secrets.
Return to Joshua Tree alone. This time
ignore everything but the sky.
Things are slower now, colder.
The stars overhead are gone now,
or maybe the clouds have rolled in,
but either way you can't see them,
can't remember how they burned.
But what you have now is infinite,
the spaces between hearts
expanding, e x p a n d i n g, e   x   p   a   n   d   i   n   g
until the only one you have left is your own.

ZOONOTIC

BEN NARDOLILLI

A family of wolves sits and waits in the neighborhood,
rumors of an empty city excite them,
the inner movements I take between these walls, I'm convinced,
are keeping them and their teeth at bay, slight vibrations
I send out to the floors, the walls, and the ceiling
which then radiate into the winds that can carry the sound away

I'm fortunate to live in this oasis of wind. In a still land,
these efforts would not travel, and who knows
what kinds of animals would start dragging their hungry bellies
down the streets of the cityscape I call home?
Already I can see the pigeons strutting about, stretching out
over the sidewalks, pink talons unafraid of human disturbance.

EVIDENCE OF ANNIHILATION

JAMES MORENA

None of us flinched or gasped when the man in the gray suit crushed the bat. We had been gathered about it, chins to chests, hands dangling by hips, sweat dripping from brows, just gazing at its furry presence in downtown Austin. Maybe the older woman with the fanny pack beside me had wondered: How did the bat get here? Maybe the woman in waist-high jeans, and a tucked-in, buttoned-up shirt had wondered: Should we call someone? The man in cargo shorts and tourist T-shirt who stood between me, and the high-jeans woman, probably had stood there thinking about Texas barbeque like many folks who visit Austin are wont to do. But the gray-suited man had side stepped around one of us before he slammed, I believe, his size 12-inch foot to the concrete before any of us had a chance to voice our initial fascinations.

I, however, just stared at the carnage. I had no thoughts about the gray-suited man's motives because the stomping reminded me of that famous milk-drop photograph, where a single drop of milk had created a stunning milk crown. Instead, I wondered how many bats would have been needed to be splattered for the milk photographer to have perfectly captured the crowning of bat blood before it forever stained the sidewalk we all stood upon.

The gray-suited man lingered after murdering the bat. No one made eye contact with him. No one looked at him. No one broke their silence to question his reason for disrupting our playground-like circle, as if we were by the swings staring at little Johnny's dropped ice cream, with his trample so hard that it reverberated a mixture of crunching bones and the wonderful symphonic clicking of the heel of well-made Italian dress shoes.

I turned to look at the older, fanny-packed lady to my left. She had trained her eyes on the high-jeans woman who stood across from her. The high-jeans woman clutched the cargo-shorted man's elbow.

For a moment, I wondered if they had been strangers before the stomping incident and if in some strange way, they would be tied together for life by this singular event. And then years from now their grandchildren would ask them to tell them about that story; that fabulous story, the one they had heard every Thanksgiving dinner, about that one time when that man with those Italian shoes bit the head off that huge fruit bat from Asia because the story would have changed as their memory of the event would have amalgamated into something far from its original form.

I soon returned to my senses when I noticed that they each wore a silver wedding band, which means they were likely already married and would later fight over who knew more details about the brisket the man ate for lunch.

I didn't look at the gray-suited man, but I could feel him sizing each of us up one at a time. It felt as if he wanted someone to challenge him, to shout at him with angry tears in their eyes, to cock back their arm then let loose a fury of punches that asked: why and how and what's wrong with you? While he stared at us, I admired his Italian shoe, the weapon of his destruction.

There was a blood spot that had somehow strayed where I imagined the second toe in a 12-inch shoe would have fit. And I wondered if the gray-suited man's second toe extended beyond his big toe, but my thoughts returned to that blood: how did it manage to land there? The man had stamped straight down, almost mechanical in precision, when he had murdered that bat. So, the laws of physics would have prevented that drop from circling around the tip of his Italian shoe to land where we all could see it. I sighed in such a loud manner that I feared everyone knew that I had so many questions about my own knowledge of physics.

I then began to wonder if the gray-suited man had killed some other creature just prior to killing our now smashed bat. Perhaps a bird, cat, or lizard. I imagined him spending his days treading on things that groups of people had gathered to appreciate: flowers, historical markers, street performers. I wondered if he would have mashed little Johnny's ice cream if it had lay before us instead.

The high-jeans woman, without a word, clumsily turned then strolled away, and I lost my train of thought. The cargo-shorted man beside her turned too, but he held his stare a bit longer on the spattered bat before his eyes were forced to follow his beer belly. The older fanny-packed woman beside me seemed relieved, unbinding her shoulders from her neck, by the others' departure as though she had been waiting, wanting, for permission to leave the scene of a crime.

The man in the gray suit gazed at me for a second longer before clicking and clacking away. I continued to stare at his Italian shoes for evidence—feathers, fur, scales—of annihilation. But his shoes were finely made, so there was nothing left to see.

BIRDSONG

MITCHELL SOLOMON

a swarm of sparrows
in the vacuum of space
violent fluttering towards no end
not that there was one in mind
claws scraping against
black throats and crowns
tearing feathers and eyes
and beaks from chestnut bodies
wings thrashed nude
oh to be lucky enough
to find a stone or tree
in this vast expanse
perch for a while
heal

HOW TO WRITE ACCIDENTS

KAYLA KING

In response to the birds beyond the window, you explore
ideals once bestowed before bed. Long lost rarities,
those words no longer sound like your father

because you can't remember
his voice. And without the din of rain,
thinking remains shrill.

He left nectarines on the counter
that morning. He bought them to keep his own
stubble, he said, scratching a hand over his jaw.

And he rinsed the skin in the sink. Even now
when water glints against the counter, you recall
how tender he was with the washing.

How careful. How sure. You knew this denotation
of lineage would only promise a family
someday, to underwhelm this version of perfection

you speak to the chins of your
lovers. Incantatory hush halts a haphazard haze
of would-be-tomorrow. If only.

You will be brutal now because you were ruined
by the thought that good fathers lived longer
than bad men who suffered in stories.

Yours lived
only thirty-seconds
more.

Now the birds are back to batter at the beveled glass
until you listen. They say forget
the imposition. Immerse only in the indulgence

of an open window while the sky shreds
itself to something far more elemental
than an Everyman could explain. Right there,

they say, that pit, encased in flesh and juice
and sweet sour blood, right there those
peaches, are they ready for the slaughter?

Rub a hand against a naked chin, think
only of picking fuzz from your teeth in a bite,
not a replica of death, but a vignette

juxtaposed against such nonsense.
The birds will come
again. They always do.

UNINVITED

MARIANNE BREMS

Wherever I go,
even with the door secured behind me,
worldliness slips in,
uninvited,
with its headstrong disbelief
that I don't want to be disturbed.
The wholeness of my dermis,
the shapes on the backs of my eyelids,
unable to prevent this invasion

of a relentless military gray sky,
excluding me from endless blue,

of the growing leak
calling to me from my faucet,

of ants feasting on sugar in my cupboard
while moths devour cornmeal,

of blood seeping from my foot
after my favorite cup breaks on the floor,

of my window stunning, perhaps wounding,
a dove that now lies motionless on the ground.

These intrusions,
wrap their tentacles
around me like a hungry tongue
eager to slide under a closed door
to swallow my peace.

THE WAY

MARGARET KOGER

Holding my breath
    in the hollow of my chest
    where stale air lingers
    lungs wait to expand

The way
    fall follows the fleeing sun
    winter wraps a chill around
    grass greens in the spring

The way
    mountain crags crumble
    rivers rendezvous
    tides follow the moon

How deer hold
    barely breathing
    See? Who are you?

How dogs bark
    warning intruders
    saving our bodies
    not saving our lives

How Mama's smile
    lit her face and mine

Holding my breath because—

The way
    I knock on wood, but
    can't find my other shoe.

21 YEARS

MEGHAN MALACHI

with a head bop to "New Thang"
by French Montana and Remy Ma

what a blessing
to be from the city
that gave us
big pun
& in part, luther vandross
& alfredo thiebaud, who soothed our homesickness with fresh coco
   while others feared our hunger
& big pun
& adolescent mouths crutched on mad and odee
& a tongue that makes us say *ball* like one of hair is rolling up
   out of our throats
& chairback clashing and tall stacks at pelham bay diner
& belcalis
& remy ma
& the payless on southern boulevard that's been going out of business
   for a decade
& the conway we bought 3 dollar panties from on hunts point
& a knowing that celebration is in order at the uttering of *vamo pa city island?*
& bodega cashiers who watched us grow up as we watched them grow old
& a hospital we were taught to trust with bullet wounds and nothing else
& mary j
& deli windows plastered with high-definition shots of food you've never
   actually seen inside
& a pride that has us lookin' sideways at anyone who claims to be the hood
& bodies leaned back for days
& lesandro
& a beach for which our love is complicated, nostalgic, and without argument:
   redamancy
& a story we thought we might loathe but now tell with a light which is
   undeniable and which is ours.

THE RABBIT, THE OWL, AND THE NEWT

RACHEL A.G. GILMAN

Over the next forty-eight hours, Susannah needed packaging tape and a man in New York willing to have sex with her. So far, she'd secured the former.

Susannah was supposed to be in Dublin. She'd never done a big spring break, but had wanted to treat herself senior year. After booking a unicorn-like $74 round-trip flight, she'd planned to wake up on St. Patrick's Day in a student hostel and embark on a pub-crawl with the mission to rid herself of her virginity before graduation, ideally to a bloke that liked Guinness and went by Shamus or Cormac. Then, a pandemic happened.

Now she found herself trying to fit four years of her life into two large cases, two carry-ons, and some cardboard boxes stolen from the recycling closet. She reached into the back of her closet and pulled out a bottle of champagne stolen from a fundraiser during her internship at the Guggenheim. She pulled the cork and drank straight, bubbles piercing her lips and spilling on the floor. The university had requested in an email that morning that all dormers depart New York. Classes had moved online over the past week as a precaution, but now the panic button had been struck. If the university was determined to kick her out, Susannah figured they didn't care if she left things a bit sticky.

The end of undergrad wasn't sad for Susannah. She'd never had much of a social life, too busy keeping up her grades to keep her scholarship, following a plan of internships for a decent job. Her busyness had largely meant avoiding boys, getting her orgasms from the Rabbit-style vibrator her sister, Kitty, had given her when she'd left for school. Her lack of experience in bed had never been important until this last semester when she'd become strangely restless, hence the Dublin plan. The more champagne she sipped, the more Susannah realized just how much solace she had in plans, how they'd all fallen mute.

Susannah finished her packing (and all of the champagne) and rewarded herself with leftover Thai food from her mini-fridge. She struggled to get fried rice onto chopsticks as she scrolled through her phone. Every time she logged onto Facebook or Instagram or Twitter, it was the same videos of people giving themselves haircuts and making bread and wondering how long it'd be before they were unemployed. It felt like being stuck at a never-ending cocktail party where everyone had forgotten to take their Zoloft.

The only content that compelled her came from Neville Goldstein, a guy she'd met in an elective class on the representation of mental health in art. He had longish brown hair that fell in a wavy tuft above his right eye over a pair of silver, circular glasses and wore t-shirts with torn jeans and heavy-looking green shoes. Susannah had thought he was gorgeous, too gorgeous for her to even think of talking to, so instead she'd tried to show she thought he was hot by clapping really loudly after he gave his final presentation on the unhealthy attitudes toward sexual relationships in rap songs. Her sophomore (and sophomoric) brain thought this would work. It hadn't. They parted ways when the semester ended and never crossed paths, except for online, after Susannah had added him on Instagram: @nevgoldie. His posts were mostly shaky concert photos. Susannah hadn't paid attention until he shared the music videos.

Nev's songs were inspired by his time in impending quarantine. His first one was about his houseplants. He walked around his apartment barefoot in a white tank top and matching linen trousers, singing into his iPhone. Sometimes the phone was mounted so he could pose, chapped lips pouted, holding his vintage Fender and serenading his succulents. He stroked their leaves and at one point came comically/uncomfortably close to kissing a ficus. Susannah had sat in her twin XL bed the past few nights finishing a can of Pringles and re-watching the video. Of its 178 views, she was accountable for half. She was even more drawn in by his most recent creation, 'expired lettuce [lofi]', where he cleaned out his refrigerator contents, feigning emotion at what had to be disposed of and ending the whole production with a black screen, *Rest in Peace* superimposed followed by a list of discarded food.

Susannah champagne-dizzily commented on the videos. She left red heart emojis (the one that lives with the playing card symbols rather than with the other hearts; more interesting) and wrote: *you are the gift the world doesn't deserve right now* and *I want to turn you into a milkshake and pour you into my mouth*. It felt right in the moment, the one before she passed out.

On St. Patrick's Day, Susannah awoke to bagpipes. Her dorm faced Fifth Avenue where a small collective of elderly white men had gathered with Irish flags, distanced from one another and holding something like a parade in the rain. Susannah sat up, clenching her pounding forehead and checking her phone. 12:04 PM. There were news updates from CNN and the *New York Times* announcing the Met Gala had been postponed and India had closed down its film industry. A new email from the university told them they wanted to know where they were going the rest of the semester so they could track possible cases, which felt antithetical to sending them home. Most notably, there was an Instagram notification from @nevgoldie.

Haha thx for all the luv, Nev wrote, *hows it goin?*

Susannah sat up. It had come in twenty minutes ago, enough time that she could answer and still seem cool. *I'm fine, just waiting for the world to end. How about yourself?*

The phone beeped with another notification: Nev asking if she wanted to FaceTime.

Susannah attempted to make herself presentable, flattening her fluff of hair, smacking her cheeks to force color into them. She responded, *sure*, with her number.

Shortly after, Nev appeared on her iPhone screen, her blurry reflection in the lenses of his glasses. He touched his face, drawing Susannah's attention to his neckbeard. He was at an angle that made it look like he was sticking his head out of a car to order at a fast food drive-thru.

"Hey," he said, hair in his eyes. "What's up?"

"Uh, not much," Susannah replied. "What's up with you?"

"Oh, you know," he said. She didn't have a clue. "Wanted to thank you for liking my videos. Means a lot that someone other than my sister watches." He laughed. "We had class together, right?"

Susannah nodded.

Nev licked his lips. "Anyone ever call you Susie?"

"Hardly ever," she said. "Well, actually, no, not at all." The name was so foreign to her that she was uncertain what kind of a Susie she'd even be: one with an *ie,* or with a *y*?

"What are you doing?" Nev asked. "You live in Brooklyn?"

"I'm packing up my dorm room," Susannah said. "I leave tomorrow."

"Oh," Nev replied. "Well, are you free?"

Susannah stared at Nev through her iPhone. Maybe this was a plan. "Sure," she said.

Nev smiled. He invited Susannah to his place near Prospect Park. Susannah hadn't been to Brooklyn much over her four years in the city. It was where the social butterflies tended to flock. She had no idea where Prospect Park was; let alone how to get there. She decided despite the rain to bike. It was the mode of transportation that was the least likely to bring judgment, to not make her feel like she had to explain to passers-by that she was trying to tick off *sex* on her to-do list before it became impossible to touch anyone.

Her ride took her past many Irish pubs. At stoplights, Susannah looked at their shamrock chains hanging from the ceilings and leprechauns with pots of gold painted in the windows. She felt nostalgic despite never having been inside. She peddled across the Manhattan Bridge, watching as people in masks multiplied.

Nev had agreed to meet her outside the Whole Foods in Gowanus. He said it was near his place and Susannah liked that she could always bail and get groceries. She pulled up to the curb outside and saw a line curling around the block, people leaving the length of a basketball player between them as suggested by bright orange cones, scanning their phones. Susannah did and didn't want to know the latest, how far past 100 the death toll had risen over thirty minutes.

"Yo, Susie!"

Susannah's eyes worked their way around until she noticed someone waving across the street. A man in a yellow rain slicker with green Doc Marten brogues walked toward her. Susannah assumed it was Nev, but he had something covering his face. As he came closer, she saw it was an elephant mask with a large, plush trunk attached. She rolled her bike toward him and they met in the middle of the sidewalk a few feet apart.

41

"Hey," he said, the sound muffled. His glasses were steamed, covered in rain splotches. "I'm this way." He pointed and Susannah started wheeling her bicycle. The neighborhood was uphill and it was hard to breathe in the rain. Eventually, Nev stopped in front of a brick townhouse. Susannah shoved her bike between trash cans, hoping it looked less enticing to steal.

The home was set up railroad style. The living room had lamps with green light bulbs and an old, tweedy couch. "We put them in for that Halloween party," Nev said, leaving his mask and shoes at the door. "Did you come to that?"

Susannah slipped off her soaked shoes. She had no idea what he was talking about.

Nev cleaned his glasses on his t-shirt. "Can I get you a drink?"

Susannah nodded and followed him into the kitchen. The countertop was filled with empty cardboard Budweiser boxes and should-have-been-refrigerated condiments. Nev pulled out a dented beer can, explaining a roommate had been gifted the beer at his wait staff job before heading out of town. Nev was the only one around because his parents were old and he didn't want to risk it, plus he preferred the quiet. Susannah listened and looked at her beer, wishing the scene she'd hung out in the past four years had taught her to voluntarily drink carbonated wheat.

Nev sipped from his can dramatically, arching his back and sticking out his stomach so he looked pregnant with a baby possum. "I'm actually working on a new song. I keep my music stuff upstairs," he said. "Want to hear it?"

"Oh," Susannah said, surprised and disappointed despite having been the one to send a message asking for his milkshake in her mouth. "Okay."

They climbed the staircase to his bedroom. It was smaller than it'd looked in the video, hardly large enough to fit the Queen-sized bed in the center, the same generic IKEA frame and white sheets every twenty-something was sold when they went to the store in Red Hook. The only difference was it had pillows that could've been pinched from a hotel with a 2-star review, the kind Susannah convinced herself had always been beige. The walls were plain aside from a small television and a framed *Cheers* poster. The nicest thing by far was the light-colored wooden desk in the corner with two laptops sitting like art pieces: a Dell and a Mac. Susannah wondered if it'd be better to fuck there. It felt classier, she thought, as she considered strewing across it.

Nev set his beer can down and tripped over a sneaker before getting his acoustic guitar. "Okay, so," he said, falling onto the bed, "I'm thinking about, like, working on something maybe about my shower."

"Your shower?" Susannah said. She turned inside the doorway toward the mess supposed to be the closet.

Nev nodded. "Yeah, or maybe just the curtain," he said. "It's kind of shiny and shit, and I think it'd be a good metaphor, for like, covering up pain with beauty, especially if I do an EDM thing." He plucked a few guitar strings; Susannah figured just enough to prove he could play.

She looked closer at the closet. T-shirts in various colors spilled out. It was hard to tell what was on them. She touched one. It was scratchier than she imagined. Unfolding it, she revealed a faded Hooter's logo, a foolish owl staring at her average chest.

"Susie?" Nev asked, still strumming. "What do you think?"

Susannah dropped the t-shirt and the unopened beer can. "Uh," she said. "Why limit yourself to your house? Go outside, around the corner, or even, maybe, inside yourself." She watched Nev reach for a notebook, scribbling the gibberish coming out of her mouth. "Or, whatever," she said, bending down to pick things up. "I don't really know."

Smiling, Nev set the guitar down. "No, you do."

Susannah then sat next to Nev. Their eyes flitted around the other's face before her body started falling forward. Nev moved, too, closing his eyes as if he was going to kiss her then opening his entire mouth like someone had offered him a submarine sandwich. His breath smelled like weed and cocktail sauce, bringing Susannah's mind back to all of the freeze-dried fish she'd watched him sort in the refrigerator video. She tried to lean into it. At least his mouth was warm, undoing her rain-soaked body. She wondered if her fingertips felt cold as she touched his shoulder, if he even noticed.

They made out for a while. Susannah hadn't done so since middle school. It was as she remembered, like having a small fish flop against her teeth.

43

"Do you want to turn some music on?" Nev asked in between. He ran his hand down the side of Susannah's body and it was ticklish, the way she felt when the doctor gave her a gastric organ exam, and routine, like Nev had practice.

Susannah slid her hand onto the comforter. "Uh…" She wondered if Nev was the sort of dude that got off to his own, auto-tuned voice. "Let's put something on TV."

Nev stood up and found the remote. The tiny flat screen illuminated with Cartoon Network as Nev struggled to get the buttons to cooperate. After some grunting, he moved through channels, lingering on National Geographic and Food Network, speeding past the serial killer movie marathon on Lifetime.

"Wait, stop," Susannah said when she saw the CNN logo.

Nev smirked. "Really?" he said. "Wolf Blitzer does it for you?"

Susannah didn't reply.

Nev tossed the remote to the side and turned toward his dresser. He had a clear cookie jar perched on the corner, the sort that women where Susannah grew up normally filled with snickerdoodles or, in less kind homes, oatmeal raisin. Nev's contained bright-colored condoms. Susannah had initially mistaken them for candies. He picked up the jar and brought it over, opening the lid and wiggling his eyebrows. "Lady's choice," he said, like a waiter at Johnny Rockets offering a straw from a canister. Susannah plucked out a silver one that said *SENSITIVE*. Nev set down the jar, then returned to bed, pressing his mouth against Susannah's again as he moved on top of her.

Susannah looked around his head to see the news headlines. She had to smooth his hair out of the way, which he mistook for flirtation, moaning into her ear before kissing her collarbone as she squinted at the ticker running along the bottom. Some of the updates she'd seen—countries all over the world closing their borders; hotels, shops, and restaurants all over the country closing their doors; a global recession looking likely—but some had broken in the past few hours.

New studies showed the virus was able to live on surfaces for up to three days. The global death toll had surpassed that in China alone, cases rapidly ballooning in Italy. Navy ships might send support for New York as Governor Cuomo tried to convince the President of

44

the state's dwindling stockpile. The stockpiles were dwindling everywhere.

Susannah continued to watch as Nev undressed, barely registering he was trying to help her out of her own clothes.

When Nev took off his glasses, he lost some of his magic, but Susannah tried not to care too much as they got under the covers. Taking the condom from the nightstand, he asked, "Are you good with this?"

Susannah nodded, waiting for him to get wrapped and enter her before turning her attention back to Blitzer.

It wasn't what Susannah had expected. Nev's naked, hairy body felt like having a heated, weighted pillow on top of her that also breathed in her ear. His penis felt less like her rabbit toy and more like a newt, small and a tad clumsy, struggling to find her G-spot, or her clit, or a rhythm. He was trying to be gentle, she figured, as he mumbled into her neck.

The whole event lasted the course of an interview Blitzer did with the owner of a curry shop in Kips Bay that was worried about closing permanently and part of a commercial break, concluding when Nev came in the middle of an ad for a toothpaste brand that claimed it was going to be there to support people through these difficult times.

He held her through the next segment where Blitzer announced that cases of COVID-19 had officially been found in all fifty states. Then Susannah closed her eyes.

She realized she'd fallen asleep when she woke up and saw Nev had dried and folded her rain-soaked clothes. He sat next to them on the end of the bed with a beer, wearing a clean t-shirt. CNN was still on but Don Lemon had taken over.

"This whole thing," Nev said, motioning toward the television. "When do you think it'll be normal?"

Susannah got out of bed. "No idea," she said, struggling to pull her tight jeans over her stomach. "I won't find a job, though."

"What'd you study?" Nev asked.

"Art history."

"Well, I mean, to be fair, you were always kind of screwed, right?" Nev pushed his glasses up the bridge of his nose and Susannah noticed he had a tattoo behind his ear, a fish. She'd somehow missed it when hooking up; too busy with Wolf. He stood up from the bed. "Do you want me to call you an Uber?"

"I have my bicycle."

"Oh, yeah." Nev downed his beer. "Well, I guess I'll walk you out," he said, stepping out of his room and tripping over the shoe that paired with the one he'd tripped on earlier.

Alone, Susannah frowned at the sweater in her hands. She turned back to Nev's closet and picked up the Hooter's shirt, slipping it over her head before she finished dressing and went downstairs. Her sneakers were still sopping wet but she tried to pretend it didn't matter as she knotted the laces around her feet. It was getting particularly dark out with the rain. She wished she was already back in Manhattan.

"So, do you want to keep in touch when you, like, get settled back home?" Nev asked. "I would be into more of your musical input."

The idea of Nev FaceTiming Susannah in her conservative parents' kitchen, listening to him talking through a ballad about his coffeemaker before pulling out his small veiny dick to jerk off into his webcam enticed no part of Susannah's brain. Still, looking down at her sloshy sneakers, she shrugged. "Sure," she mumbled. It was another sort of a plan.

Nev smiled, leaning in and pecking her on the mouth. He then opened the door and waved goodbye. Susannah could hear the sound of the lock turning over the dulled sprinkle before she managed to take off.

The ride back to her dorm was difficult to navigate despite there being even less traffic than there had been that afternoon. Susannah expected to see green plastic hats and shamrock glasses littering the streets from parties but instead she passed forgotten paper masks and stray latex gloves. The scratchy Hooter's t-shirt moved against her skin uncomfortably as she rode and her neck itched from where Nev's neckbeard had rubbed against it, though she figured no one she passed noticed her discomfort or could tell she'd finally had sex and was now on her way home to embrace her rabbit and finish the job. There were other things to consider.

She decided to take the Brooklyn Bridge back, figuring more people might be on it. She didn't want to be alone yet. As she got closer to Manhattan, Susannah saw a massive rain cloud hanging over the island. She stopped for a minute, looking at the city. The big buildings stood tall and the lights shone brightly. It really seemed like any other typical spring day.

THE BRIDGE

JUSTIN MAHER

I've noticed hay fancies your sweaters. Gold sticks mar your perfect
wool warmth. In all the epochs of your sweaters since leaving the fields

and balers, the hay always finds you, when in range.
Never doesn't. Never hasn't.

Trace tells me I met you before. In a kitchen, first.
Personally, I don't remember,

although you do seem like someone like me;
someone who *would*, given opportunity.

There are some words which when spoken have the power
to rip a piece of your crisping tree in two. Or three.

I'm losing balance, true. I took so much more from you.
And now I can't even say I want to keep this.

Trace says you loved me in that one commercial
on the Brooklyn Bridge. I was not meant to be in any commercial,

but I went jogging that day, made my way
across the bridge; fate ran me through the back of the

shot, under beamish metal bones above,
trespassing onto a private shoot,

shouting at pigeons, "I have to get to the other side."
I guess they went for it as I am now in a commercial for bridges.

At the end of the bridge was a man with a stand displaying
his array of rope-wrapped jewelry and there I saw it.

The splendorous bindings might be blinding to the peasant eye
but I have people on the inside just for that.

I knew exactly who to give this necklace to. I knew whose collarbone
was bred for this whittled beechwood balancing in wrapped yarn

from yak hairs, or maybe twine. When I give it to her,
Trace will thank me and cry because she knows it can never leave her

neck and her albino balinese will lean into my leg,
purring with wide eyes and a closed mouth.

Our ventriloquist is a veterinarian by night.
Scratch that. Switch those. He told me this one day

while I was choosing the hours for my cat's pending de-fertilization.
He was working on a character who was a somber, non-sober feline

whose catchphrase casually involved the word *litter*.
His laugh smelled like burnt coffee scented tobacco.

Thinking of the snowy cat who will purr at my feet reminds me to go
feed my own. So I buy the necklace and leave,

continuing my jog before catching the B25.
I should've stopped and bought you a lint roller.

5 A.M. CONVERSATIONS WITH A FRIEND

PAM R. JOHNSON DAVIS

Alright, alright.
I hear you.
You are always willing to provide your feedback.
Loudly, might I add.
But I don't love you any less.
It's just not realistic.
It's not realistic
to give you more than what you need
especially when
every week,
as we sit side by side,
we hear news of layoffs at work,
or expectations that after careful inspection
there will be budget cuts.
Yet,
you meow once again.
And I sigh,
resigned,
willing to buy you
that catnip you don't need.

FOR THE HOPELESS SCROLL UNDER THE SWIPE OF YOUR FINGER

JERICA TAYLOR

Do not succumb to despair.
The bakery is hiring,
which means tomorrow, someone
will be making bread.

The scent will travel across the canal,
and down the empty street in the early morning.
You will know it in your fragile inhalation.

And if we lose this now,
we will find it again,
and we will make bread
until we run out of pans.

INDISPENSIBLE

CAROLINE TAYLOR

My brother thinks I'm out of control. I suppose there's evidence for it, but a guy's gotta make a living, doesn't he? This time, I needed help, so I asked Sandy to come with me. "There's two really cherry cycles in that garage," I told him. "Guy wants me to pick 'em up and store them at our place."

"Why?"

"Because the owner owes him money. It's a righteous kidnapping, one that doesn't involve people."

"Why do we have to go at night?" he asked me.

Sandy's questions did tend to cut right to the chase, but I couldn't tell him the real reason, so I said, "Owner works a night shift. Otherwise, he might hear us messin' around his garage and come out shooting."

I'd been told the garage door wouldn't be locked, but it was.

"Now, what do we do?" My brother's orange hair sprouted up in spikes all over, like he'd stuck his finger in a live socket. I should have done this on my own. Sandy didn't like bending the rules, let alone breaking them. "Let's check around the side," I said.

That door was also locked.

"Now what—"

"Don't say it," I cut in. "Why don't you go on back to the truck? You're making me nervous."

He crossed his arms and scowled at me. "You asked me to help you. Somebody's gotta make sure you don't do something stupid."

Sandy knew I had a tendency to take risks that landed me in trouble, as evidenced by a recent three-month stay in the county jail. But I needed him to drive getaway, not that I'd told him that. If all went according to plan, we'd be back home before dawn. If things went sideways, though, it would prove Sandy was right. Still, the reward was worth taking the chance.

"You hear that?" I said. A mewling sound was coming from behind the door.

"You told me there wouldn't be anybody here." He motioned toward the door. "Why is it locked?"

Maybe my intel (a Suzuki Hayabusa Custom Streetfighter and a 2014 Harley-Davidson Street Glide Custom Bagger, together retailing for $73,000 and ripe for the taking) was faulty. I should have known it was a little too good to be true. I took a step back, pondering my next move, the smart one being to leave. On the other hand, I'd never forgive myself for walking away from $73,000 smackers. "How about you put your hands over your eyes."

"Okay."

Pulling the set of picks from my pocket, I set to work. "Don't look now," I warned Sandy. "You could be blinded."

"Uh, Bob? Could you stop for a minute?"

"Sure."

He dropped his hands from his eyes. "I don't know what you're gonna do, bro, but I don't want to be here when you get in trouble, especially if I go blind. You mind if I go back to the truck?"

"Nope. I'm gonna try to get inside. There might be somebody in there who's hurt bad."

He turned to go. "Call me if you need me."

I held my hand out. "Gimme your phone."

"What?"

I didn't want my brother calling the cops, which he was very likely to do, thinking they would help rescue whoever was hurt when I was pretty sure that sound wasn't coming from a human being. "Gimme the phone, dammit. I might have to call 9-1-1."

The place was pitch dark inside, but I didn't need a light to see the woman standing there, pointing a shotgun at me. I froze as a tabby cat streaked past me into the night.

"Well, well, well." The voice was familiar.

Mona Hawkes.

My probation officer emerged from the shadows. "I see you're wearing gloves, Bob. Why do I doubt it has anything to do with protecting your health?"

"I see you're stockpiling paper goods," I replied. "Why do I suspect you're hoarding other supplies?"

"Needs are a must," she replied. "I'll give you the grand tour." She motioned for me to come inside.

The place didn't look like a garage; didn't smell like one either. Its walls were lined with metal shelves, and they were stuffed, floor to ceiling, with jumbo packs of toilet paper and paper towels, boxes of facial tissues of various sizes, even paper napkins. No oil stains on the concrete floor, no whiff of anything suggesting a motorcycle had ever been on the premises. "Lot a people out there could use this stuff," I said, as we reached the other side of the garage.

"Yep," she said. She nodded. "An experienced burglar like you can be very useful these days."

"I never pictured you going over to the dark side, Mona." What's in it for you? Aside from the money you'll make on the black market, that is."

"I have my reasons. Maybe I'll share them." She winked at me. "Or, I could just turn you in. Breaking and entering is a felony, Bob, as I am sure you know. Violating your probation will have you back inside real fast." She paused a moment to adjust her grip on the gun.

It had to be getting heavy, not that I had a hope in hell of snatching it away.

"And don't think you can talk yourself out of it, either. Who do you think they'd believe, hmmm?

I already knew the answer.

"My advice, Bob? Be a good boy, and you'll eventually find out what this is all about."

* * *

The first place I broke into for Mona was a piece of cake. The owner, an elderly man in his eighties, was in the orchard out back, trying to harvest what few peaches were ripe at that point. I came. I went. I felt stupid doing Mona's bidding. What was her game?

The second place was problematic. The woman had a dog and an alarm system, both of which could be dealt with, but not without me getting caught. Mona solved that by offering to take her to the post office so she could mail a package and buy stamps. While they were away, I keyed in the code Mona had got for me and then fed the dog a piece of medicated steak. He'd wake up groggy in an hour or so, but the woman probably wouldn't notice. She had some really nice jewelry in her bedroom, which I was sorely tempted to take: a diamond choker, a sapphire brooch, and a gold bangle bracelet that could be melted down to cover more than a few celebratory beers.

Unfortunately, Mona had a bad habit of patting me down after every excursion. "No freelancing," was how she put it. So I took only what she'd told me to.

The burglaries went on for weeks, mostly at night, the exception being the woman with the dog. It got to the point that things became almost routine, the most regular job I'd ever had, if you ignore the hours. Mona would case the joint, tip me to the challenges, help me surmount them if she could, and then tell me, "Go to it, Tiger."

Where she got her intel about these marks, I really don't know. Social media, most likely. One of those neighborhood chat rooms where people sound off (politics verboten), dish out advice, and sometimes brag about how they've got everything they need because they wisely stocked up.

I'd had a hard time with my brother after the botched raid. Sandy had bugged me to no end about what I found in the garage. Naturally, I lied. Not about the cat, though. I didn't want my brother thinking I wouldn't help a distressed critter.

"The place was empty." I played it as though I'd been set up, which was true. "The guy who owns those bikes must have been tipped off."

His eyes widened. "Holey moley. What about the guy who asked you to get them? Like, does he think you stole them?"

"Naw. I sent him a pic of the empty garage, even offered to let him search our garage. He's cool. Got the cops on it now." All of which was total bullshit.

"Well, darn," Sandy slapped the side of his leg. "I thought we could— you know. Like, get paid for taking the risk?"

"Don't worry about it, bro," I said, clapping him on the shoulder. "There'll be other opportunities."

Speaking of which, I was getting mighty tired of being Mona's tame burglar. Especially when there wasn't anything in it for me— except her not turning me in, that is.

"How long is this gig going to last?" I asked her one day. "I mean, haven't I done enough for you lately? I got other things to do, ya know."

"I bet you do, Bob. But I'm not finished yet, as you can tell by looking in my garage."

Without looking, I could tell nothing much was changing, thanks to me and possibly other parolees she had under her thumb. The stuff came in; the stuff went out. Same old, same old. It was both burglary and reverse burglary. Sorta like that old-time English thief whose last name was the same as what folks usually call me. "You're not taking the same risks as me," I reminded her. "One of these days, I'll get caught."

"Perhaps. But what are those damn hoarders gonna do? Call the cops?" She cracked up, laughing. "Of course, if you'd rather go back to county, just let me know. My sources inside tell me it's now a hotbed of infection."

The latest job was nearly my last. I had just squeezed through a narrow basement window and was trying to see if there were any shelves, when an elderly man in a stained polo shirt and khakis came creeping down the stairs, brandishing a pistol.

"What the hell are you doing?" He flicked on the overhead light.

"Oh." I feigned bewilderment. "This isn't Joe Anderson's place? He asked me to check on the freezer over there, make sure it was still running."

The geezer snorted. "I suppose he told you to come in through his basement window? Hah. I might be older than dirt, but I'm not an idiot."

"Okay. You got me," I pointed at the two weeks' supply of toilet paper and paper towels that I'd just tossed through the window onto the floor. "I'll just take this back, if you don't mind." I picked up one of the packages and turned to leave.

"Wait," he said, lowering the gun. "We're kind of—that is, my wife has run out. We're practically down to using newspapers, and we don't dare go to the grocery store. She's recovering from cancer, so…" his voice trailed off. The hand not holding the gun reached into his pocket as he muttered, "Least I can do." He withdrew a watch and held it out to me. "Here. It's antique. Worth quite a bit, although not nearly as priceless as this stuff."

Yeah, I was tempted, but I told him no. It wasn't so much that Mona would find the watch when she did her pat-down. It was more me thinking Sandy might be proud of me.

POWER OUTAGE

BETH BOYLAN

On the hottest night yet, the power goes. I think of sweating
in my father's old tee-shirts as a kid, the electric fans on stands
that did nothing but stir up the swampy night air.
My mother texted today; she would do so much differently if she could
have another go. But the world is ending and she's waiting for locusts.
Wear your mask and pray that you live.
I think of the mayo and Diet Coke in my fridge.
Son of Sam. Blackout '77. Grand Central
in the dark. Central Park. Five kids. Nine kids shot since
June. Stopped subways underground. Stopped elevators
midfloor. Sweltering coffins. I can't breathe. No more.
The neighbor's dog won't stop barking.
Midnight riots. My dirty sheets. City streets, cars on fire. Looking
up at acres of stars. How long before the eggs expire. Mothers are
crying. Sticky fingers. Wash your hands. Virus lingers. Men are
dying. O, manic, angry heat, just let me sleep. All the birds have
stopped singing and flown toward the moon.
Even they know to leave when the world blows its fuse.

UNTITLED
(THESE WALLS ALMOST CONTAIN YOU)

DAPHNE DAUGHERTY

these walls almost contain you

with electric lights and cool air
a rainless roof that hides the sky
the scent of linen heavy on the tongue
and smoke alarms and doorbells and
the way that we must walk to keep the floorboards from creaking

and you
barefoot in the tall grass
watching, always watching
always waiting to be exiled
wanting and dreading it in equal parts

these walls cannot contain you
these walls should not
contain you these walls will not—

let me run wild with you
show me your trails and your dens
teach me to smell joy on the wind
lead me to the creek you drink from and then

rip the breath from my lungs and the flesh from my bones
pull me to pieces and bury yourself there
give me death and give me life and
take me drag me crush me
show me how to greet the moon and then

let me curl my fingers in your hair, gentle you
let me lead you back home
hold you to my heart and whisper

STONE SILVER BIRD BLESSINGS

TRACY ROSE STAMPER

Silver lining lovers
tout blessings of perspective.
So I try. Lying down
on the driveway
I track clouds.
Get a good shiner
compliments of golf-sized hail.
The sun breaks through.
So does a fiery sunburn
reminding me
I'm alive.
Rain schools me: I discern
teardrops from raindrops
by tasting for salt.
(I'm learning
new skills, as recommended
during this time)
The asphalt gets harder
nightly.
Originally worried
about joint stiffness,
I glean that bedsores
are more pressing.
Lying here motionless,
nobody approaches.
I achieve social distancing
plus time outdoors.

RETURN OF INNOCENCE

HELEN FALLER

The kiss had been taboo.

She hadn't been touched by another adult for months. No friendly hugs, handshakes or cheek kisses in greeting or farewell. No gentle pats on the arm during conversations to emphasize a point. The result was rampant perversion. She fantasized endlessly about physical contact with random male bodies. The images floating before her eyes had been graphic and obscene. Skin, genitals, fingers, mouths, earlobes.

Reality was different.

It had felt good when Jitter Leg intertwined his fingers with hers and bit her lip. She liked his hand on the small of her back pulling her against his black-clad torso. Pleasure had coursed through her body when his mouth alighted on her neck. But the whole time she had been thinking: this is wrong, this is illegal, any of the dozens of people passing by could confront us for breaking the rules. The police should fine us. Because if we were a couple, if we had been a couple before, if we had the right to stand close like that, we wouldn't be kissing desperately by the side of the path overlooking the filthy canal littered with trash and stinking of human feces.

We'd be kissing at home.

Just a quarter-hour after the kiss, she was in the middle of traffic on Zossenerstraße by a red-brick church that had survived World War II, when she reached into her backpack for her cellphone. In disbelief, she felt again before she turned her bicycle around and pedaled furiously the wrong way along the sidewalk path, past the crumbling, graffitied walls. A few Berliners looked askance at her, but her eyes, busily scanning the ground, didn't notice them. Turning a corner, she bounced over silver cobblestones that rattled her fillings and across Kottbusser Damm to the Landwehrkanal.

Scouring the path along the canal as she rode, she tried to remember the precise place in their promenade where Jitter Leg had

61

pounced. Then she saw the floral-patterned case that had protected her phone. Someone had taken the phone but left the case. Her embroidered handkerchief was there too. Both must have tumbled out when he had pushed her up against the railing.

* * *

The pandemic had shot dating as she knew it into the brown. There was suddenly so much time, and a mandate to take things slowly, to write notes without the urgency of rushing into a tryst. She fine-tuned her online photos and spent hours mulling over what she truly wanted. She was reluctant to meet anyone in person, afraid of doing something that might cause more old people to die. The offers she received to cuddle and kiss or to massage her from head to toe made it easy to say no.

After seventy-nine days of confinement, a music journalist broke her resolve with a complaint that it was impossible to get to know her within the chat bubbles of a dating app. He proposed a perambulation through Hasenheide Park, vowing to maintain a gentlemanly distance. In their exchanges prior to meeting, they discussed inviting a chaperone and wondered where she might procure a parasol and lace gloves with all the shops closed and Amazon overwhelmed with toilet paper deliveries.

Dressed in a brocaded vest, he opened the gate for her with his elbow. As the regulations only allowed leaving home to buy necessities or to take exercise, they strode briskly with the decreed yard-and-a-half distance between them. They wore no masks.

Ascending the hill past the friendly drug dealers who plied their trade in the bushes and the zoo with its squawking peacocks, they circled the park's perimeter and tramped past the hidden pond full of paired-off ducks. He related how, while tippling absinthe in Brandenburg, he'd encountered a group of women performing a moonlight ritual to ward off the virus. Peeking at him out of the corner of one eye, she was unable to gaze fully into his face and decide, despite looking prematurely old and far too pink for her liking, if he had what it took to interest her intellectually and emotionally and the power, eventually, to stuff her pussycat in proper fashion. At last, the relentless movement ceased and they sat on adjacent benches in

62

Hasenheide's rose garden, gloriously full of possibilities, even with the tart cold in the spring air. She noted a bee dipping its tongue into a blossom and thought that perhaps he just might.

While waiting to see if the Brocaded Journalist would suggest a second date, she played the flaneuse with another man in the newspaper business. He was offended at the moment they met because she didn't shake his proffered hand, instead extending her card and observing silently that his bald spot was larger than his WhatsApp portrait divulged. She was offended later when he took off his loose smock and she could smell his musty, unwashed body and count the sparse hairs on his concave chest. This is what you have to offer me, she thought, and you can't even bathe beforehand?

Sitting side by side on a blanket he'd brought to the Tiergarten, an idyll lush with plant life and birds flourishing in the absence of cars, they argued about politics. She was unimpressed by his understanding of the economics of Berlin's housing shortage and he was insulted when she suggested that, if the Turks who sold börek at his corner bakery couldn't speak proper German, he might learn a few words of Turkish. *I choose to live in Germany and speak German*, was his indignant response. Then Musty Chest told her the lockdown should end, since the average age of those dying was eighty-eight, and they would all expire within a few months' time anyway.

When they parted ways, she concluded that experiencing the magnificence of the park's nature during the work stoppages was her gift that day. If not for the date, she wouldn't have visited it and breathed in all that fresh air and fallen even more deeply in love with Berlin's awkward beauty.

Then came Jitter Leg and the forbidden kiss.

Hoping he would be as interesting in person as he appeared in his profile, she'd told her daughter she had to pop out to the store to buy milk. He turned out to be a computer programmer who spent long days and nights with screens as his only company. His best effort at making an emotional connection had been suggesting that they engage in an Iron Maiden singalong.

"On a long and lonesome highway…," he warbled. She didn't join in.

They had already walked a distance and were sitting by the canal, watching nothing. His hand inched ever closer to hers. He wasn't worth risking infection, so she turned and explained that she wouldn't touch him because it was too dangerous.

Later though, as they were sauntering back in the direction of her bicycle, she allowed him to grasp her fingers—she could wash them as soon as she got home—and ended up against the railing. He kissed her with hopeless passion. His left leg started to tremble with desire. Dark circles of longing emerged under his eyes. He pushed his body against hers and asked her to come to his apartment. After months of sexual quarantine, his fingers and lips caused welcome stirrings. But she turned him down. He invited her again and she thought, how easy would that be? Just go rut with him and leave, go back to her own life as an intellectual single mom with a penchant for social justice.

But rutting wasn't enough anymore. At his thirty-seven years of age, Jitter Leg wasn't quite young enough to be her son, but he also wasn't far off. She could too clearly see the end of the thing in its beginning.

Now, as she bent over to pluck the phone case and hankie out of the fetid dirt, she fought the urge to think of the loss of her mobile as karmic punishment for breaking the rules the authorities had imposed to keep everyone from dying. She was awash in guilt. Kissing a stranger in the age of coronavirus felt as risky as having condomless sex with countless men.

Back home in her Altbau apartment, she borrowed her daughter's Nokia to call her cell. It rang and she left a message offering a reward. The following morning, she called again. Someone had turned the phone off.

Not having a mobile was both disorienting and wholesome. She reached for it all the time. The dating apps, the calculator, the weather. In this time of endless isolation, it was the primary way she connected to friends, family and colleagues, near at hand and around the globe. Her folly by the canal had cost her hundreds of euros and considerable chagrin. She excluded essential details when explaining to her acquaintances why she couldn't SMS.

At the same time, without the electronic distraction in hand, she was liberated from invasive messages. She felt more connected to her immediate world. The air was richer, fuller, the scent of flowers sweeter.

Yet, the feeling of self-reproach lingered.

The next day, wondering if another tryst with the Brocaded Journalist was in the offing, she turned on her computer and checked the dating site. Jitter Leg had sent several messages. "Hi" said one. A few hours later, "What's up?" and then "What are you wearing?" A corset, duh, she thought, and didn't bother to respond. Musty Chest had also sent a missive. Before their rendezvous, he'd asked to text her. Apparently he'd violated their agreement and dialed, and was shocked when a man picked up. That man had requested that Musty pass his phone number on to her.

A warm, friendly voice answered when she called the number. She was at a loss for words. Had he picked up her mobile and then decided to return it once he couldn't deduce the password?

The friendly voice told her she could find him and her phone at the flower stall in the outdoor market by the Landwehrkanal the following day. She asked his name. He seemed surprised at the question, but told her anyway: Jürgen.

He sounded comely.

The next morning, after settling her daughter in for her mathematics lesson on Zoom, she cycled to the market. Threading through the pruned-out crowds of people milling about the stalls, she barely noticed the scent of the green olives or the arresting richness of the reams of bright fabric. Finding the flower stand, she saw a boy in his late teens and asked if he were Jürgen.

"I am the son of Jürgen," he replied.

A woman around her age, long white roots showing in her bright orange hair, looked at her. "The dame with the handy."

"That's me."

"Jürgen's down there." The woman pointed with her chin. Her hands were full of bunches of flowers that she was laying out on the table in front of her. She called Jürgen's name.

He appeared out of a thronging crowd, tall and round-bellied, his long white hair in a thin ponytail, stuffing a Turkish döner into his mouth as he strolled. Noble, but neither available nor handsome.

When Jürgen handed her the Samsung, she tried to slip some folded bills into his palm.

He ignored the money.

"Are you sure it's your phone?" he asked gruffly.

"I recognize the scratches on the glass cover."

"But I need to know it's your phone. Enter the password or something."

She did and showed him.

"Would you like to see a photo of me?" She had taken plenty for her dating profile.

He shook his head.

"Do you know where I found it? Back there a few blocks." He stretched his long arm inland. "Next to the Aldi."

"I dropped it right here." She pointed toward the canal.

"You got lucky," the woman with the orange hair said. "My daughter got lucky just like that, two times she got lucky."

"I did get very lucky." She tried again to pass Jürgen the folded bills.

"I don't want your money." He frowned slightly.

"May I buy some flowers?"

His face lost its dourness.

"That's how I earn my bread."

She picked out the most expensive bunch on the table, creamy pink tulips with serrated white edges. The orange-haired woman wrapped them in paper and placed fifty cents change in her palm from the ten-euro bill. She thanked the family of flower sellers, thinking how fortunate she was to live in a city where people cared more for the fate of hapless strangers than they did for large monetary rewards. Placing the flowers in her bicycle basket, she lingered by the canal a moment, noticing first a regal swan swimming down its center, and then turning to enjoy the vibrant mix of people.

Arriving home, she logged onto the dating site and saw that Jitter Leg had unmatched her and disappeared. Musty Chest was annoyed she hadn't called him back and soon followed suit. The Brocaded Journalist she saw again and then told to get lost after he berated her for an hour for not being enamored of masculinist singer-songwriters.

But she didn't need any ersatz Romeos. She had the city of Berlin, looking after her even when she didn't look after herself.

THE DISTANCE IS HARROWING.
THE TEMPERATURE IS MILES.

COREY MILLER

Swelter forces the covers off, forming a mountain range of bedsheets and blankets between us. The weather throws a changeup every winter, granting a glimpse into the future.

In the past, we ventured out; hiking new trails as soon as our apps would alert us, widening our thirst for wilderness. Our circumferences were expanding, driving past the loops we began on, reaching for altitude. *As close to the sky as we can get,* you would say, *close to the sky.*

We allow the wintry exterior to sequester our adventures. Permitting the streams to slow stagnant while holding up the fort. Animals hibernate to conserve energy for low intake. You've been sheltering your thoughts, making me work to get in; tunneling through the world and falling at your knees.

Our bed feels California King. Rigid, unable to sense each other's movements throughout the night. Tonight, I fidget; restless. Perspiration pursuing to cool me down—to river me away. I crave the past: Stretching into each other. Colliding upwards. Peaking simultaneously.

You say the paths blurred, sledging through gorges and ridges that never alter, same swallow nests and decollate snails waiting for us to pass. Left to right the errors cracked within fossilized bone. I pitch a rock in the stream and claim I changed history.

You remain a cave—shifting with the mountains. Plain grazers wouldn't know these mounds are only foothills to us. *Only foothills,* you say, stepping off the path, tamping down growth.

I span the distance and scratch the bridge of your nose while you dream, the cartilage pliable and forgiving under compression. You snore and divulge in your sleep. *Climb climb climb.* Your fleshy lips are ledges to the quarry of teeth. Moss and algae and lichen grow symbiotically in a shaded moist environment, yet, they need oxygen. I slip into the gaps and crevices, exploring. The alarm clock ticks like a chisel, chipping an artificial hold into the sediment. Considering the ways one can conceal an artifact, you must tamper until there are no more Xs on the map.

LOVESICK

TINA ANTON

My garden is lovesick. You can see it in the brown spots peeking through stunted leaves. Bulbous heads, layered in a dozen silken colors, loll against the washed-out sunlight and drip petals like blood on the earthen floor. My chest aches with it.

I try to feed the garden with my own love. Self-care sparks a little growth in the healthiest plants, but it is not enough to stop the new transplants from failing. My eyes droop with bone-deep exhaustion.

Maybe this is the end of my garden; love killing the one thing born of it.

Her touch would send the tulips fluttering in delight. Now they wilt under the weight of my melancholy.

My fingers dance across the cellphone in my pocket. Her number is in there, and she would come if I called. If she knew what was happening to my garden, there would be no stopping her from helping.

I deny myself the comfort and instead curl up among the bamboo shoots and majesty palms. Their fronds settle on my shoulders, a feathery embrace.

Digging into my grief, I sit with my legs pulled up to my chest, arms wrapped around them. I hold in tears, afraid that if they finally fall, it might drown the succulents.

She left because I stupidly told her to go. Now I know it was a misunderstanding, but apologies are impossible for me. They feel like clawed fingers tearing into the dirt, squeezing bulbs until all the moisture drips out over shiny nails, plant pulp smeared across a dirty palm. The thought twists my stomach.

Tremors build in my arms and legs as my eyes close, lids too heavy to drag open.

I should call her.

The phone sits heavy in my pocket.

The bitter scent of rot rises from the moss in the corner. I grimace and burrow my face between my jeans and breasts.

I will rest and gather my strength before I try more self-assurances.

"Daisy?"

I jerk my head up, vision fuzzy for a moment. How much time has passed? The shadows seem more profound.

She stands in the gateway to my garden, hands clenched in her pockets. Her face betrays her worry, brow pinched. There is understanding in her kind brown eyes.

Longing bubbles up in my chest, and I push back further into the plants, hoping they might hide me.

She walks forward and kneels at my side.

"Daisy," she repeats my name. There is no anger. No blame. Only gentle reassurance. "It's going to be okay."

Out of the corner of my eye, I see a rosebud begin to unfurl from the retreat of its tight self-hug. Tears dampen my cheeks and I swallow, but it does nothing to clear the thickness in my throat.

She brushes the dampness away with her thumb and presses her forehead against mine so I can share her air.

The smell of rot recedes, replaced with lilac, lavender, and mint.

A laugh shakes loose from my chest. I hug her close. Her heat warms me to the marrow, and I revel in it even as guilt bobs to the surface.

"I know," she says, before I can find the words. Her hand cups my cheek. "I love you." Her lips tremble. "I love our garden. I love our life together. Will you let us try again?"

I look around at our garden. It shakes off the sickness, but evidence of my pride still lingers in the browned, curled edges of the many leaves. It will take time to return their luster. I bite my lip, clinging to shame. This close, I search her face for a hint, hope for her forgiveness.

When she smiles, the plants heave in a collective gasp of relief. We watch them begin to track the low pools of sunlight, chasing the life-giving energy they have been denied.

My fingers entwine hers like roots. "I'd like that."

70

REBUILDING WONDERLAND

PRESTON SMITH

I want to renew my vows where lemon trees grow
and the sun seldom sleeps

a fantasy world devoid of myself
until I've learned to love again

the bioluminescence of life
lavender as the twilight that introduced us

in middle school, queer exploration
conquests to see who might mark my territory

first, a glimmer of hope and adolescent love
then, a single tear at the lemon tree

to water its roots so it might grow
and keep in touch with itself always

IN CHORUS

LOUIS FABER

Deep in a small forest,
a murmuring brook reflects
the shards of sun sliding
through the crown of pines,
its whispered wisdom
infinitely more clear
than the babbling of men
holding the reins firmly
in distant cities of power.

The birds know this well,
sing of it in chorus, nature's
music, jazz scatting that
the graying clouds absorb,
an always willing audience,
and the wind rushing by
cries through the trees
in the voice of long dead
poets whose words offer
a truth to which cloistered
talking heads have grown deaf.

THERE ARE SOME CROWS OUT THERE LOSING THEIR COMPOSURE.

JUSTIN MAHER

Some of my better friends still have hybrids, and hypothetically
they will be there for me. I just don't like to ask.
Instead, I mask what I don't know with a quick
turn to what I do. I'm seeing now even that's dwindling.

Does the sketch of a mind as a sieve ring a bell?
I thought I had a bowl that was reaching capacity,
but what I have is a chipped rim instead and it's cracking farther,
further down and more is falling out with the new pushing in.

It's getting to be a savage way of learning, facing the narrative
of your today and tomorrow, while you try to remember
the last several feral yesteryears. If that's true, where are we now
on the scale? We're in someone else's idea of future,

but we still haven't perfected it. Or
maybe we have and the crowding crows flying over outside
are just holographic stimuli calling out.
Trying to convince us to watch from the window.

It/ is/ still/ possible to feel the rain outdoors if you stretch
your hand past the window's gate. Or is it window gates?
These days I can't quite hear how the birds say it. Might be
a faulty, exposed audio cord. Water damage be damned!

I reach out for the rain. Half of me wishes for some good glitches,
at least! Make me laugh. Teach me love. But please,
throw your dice at other birds. I like these ones. When they fly to the
block's end, I swear they look back and wave, smiling.

THE ELVES AND THE SHOE DESIGNER

J.S. BOWERS

Recently I traveled from the Azerbaijan State Oil Academy, by invitation, to tour the fully automated petroleum processing facility at Fospey Industries in Grendel Hills, United States. Due to pandemic restrictions, I was not able to find childcare for my young daughter, and I was forced to bring her with me. I hoped it would be acceptable if I put her in a stroller and kept her at my side throughout the visit, but my colleague at Fospey suggested that she should stay with the office's receptionist robot, which is named Bar Bar.

Bar Bar is a sleek, multi-appendaged mechanical creature who looks like nothing I have ever imagined or dreamed. She has a huge round head ("head" only because it has been assembled at the top) bouncing about on a flexible alloy support tube. In a friendly human voice, Bar Bar reassured me that she was certified for childcare and any emergency situation.

The robot then rearranged several of her parts, along with blankets and pillows, to create something I might describe as a lap or a fort. I left my little Khadiya with her and I went off to spend the day touring the factory with Thackeray Tennyngton-Griffolds Helspeth, a Fospey senior executive. It was an enlightening day for my research into solvents, but that is not why I came to write this.

After I returned to Baku on the Caspian Sea in Azerbaijan, Mr. Helspeth sent me a logged recording of Bar Bar's time spent with Khadiya. In a spirit of curiosity, I opened the file. I discovered that the Bar Bar robot had told my daughter the following story, which I am able to recount in its exact remarkable words, thanks to this recording.

* * *

Khadiya, there once was a woman named Stella Ray, who became very wealthy as a designer of fabulous Italian shoes. She was a

74

hard worker, and a compulsive smoker. The shoe company's owner was a cruel man, and one day as he tore up Stella's designs and shouted vitriol at her, Stella had a terribly painful episode of gastric reflux and heartburn. It wasn't a real heart attack, but it was a moment of illumination for Stella, and she quit her job that very instant and stormed out of the building. The next day she flew from Milan to New York, and she resolved to write a tell-all book about her experiences in the fashion industry.

So Stella settled herself at a hotel suite in Midtown, with one entire bedroom filled up with her collection of shoes. She tried to write about her life, but she learned it was hard work, putting words into sentences and paragraphs.

She was often out on her balcony, smoking and cursing unhappily. Due to the pandemic and the quarantine restrictions imposed by Governor Cuomo, she wasn't permitted to leave her room. She hired an assistant, a gig-worker named Caro, to go out and get food and liquor and cigarettes for her. The rent on the hotel room was more expensive than she had ever expected for such a shabby place, so her money wasn't going to last forever.

One morning Stella woke in the hotel bed, feeling groggy, trying to retrieve an elusive dream. When she looked at her laptop, she found that apparently, she had completed a couple of pages the night before, but she had no memory of it.

She read over the work, but it was not in her style or voice at all. Stella thought Caro had written the pages after she, herself, perhaps had a few too many drinks and blacked out.

When her assistant came to the hotel room that day, Stella tore up the pages, which she had printed purely for the purpose of tearing them up, and yelled at her. But Caro said, "You don't pay me enough to take this kind of crap from you, and I never touched your computer, and I quit."

Stella then had to beg Caro to reconsider, and she had to double the hourly rate, which didn't help the financial situation.

The next morning, again: pages on her computer she didn't remember writing. Stella considered that she had better cut back on her drinking.

That night she stayed up late in front of her laptop, playing games and scrolling around on social media, and still the words of her tell-all book refused to gush forth from her fingers. She meant to pull an all-nighter, but sometime after midnight, she fell asleep on the lumpy hotel couch. She slept poorly, and woke early, and she had a crazy dream-memory that somebody had come into her room during the night.

She remembered two intruders, very small people, not even as tall as you, Khadiya. And they had no clothes, but their bodies were shapeless and dumpy, and you couldn't tell whether they were boys or girls. But Stella remembered these two strange individuals took her laptop off the coffee table and bounced ideas off each other, writing for a couple of hours until they said, "That's enough for tonight," and slipped out the door again.

Stella looked at her document in progress and found that the two elves had written the story about when the president of the shoe company, whose name was on the shoes, tried to forcibly kiss her at the corporate Christmas party. Stella was infuriated as she read the pages, because it wasn't written in the snarky and aggrieved tone that reflected the way she felt about the incident. All the same, though, the text was free of errors, the language was clear, and the facts were correct.

So she left it alone. Day after day, Stella struggled with her words and stories, and night after night, the two elves came and fixed the word-tangle she had left unfinished. Eventually she stopped being annoyed at the way the editor-elves toned down her angry prose, and even began to admire the quality of their work. The pages seemed to spin themselves like silk, and soon she had a completed manuscript on her laptop.

She sent a query to a high-powered New York agent, who asked to read the whole draft, and who then called Stella in a state of great excitement. She was very enthusiastic to represent the book and to negotiate a deal with a publisher. After an hour of talking, the agent said, "I just have one other question. Did you write this book yourself?"

Stella hesitated in answering, and the agent recognized this pause, and said "You had help, didn't you? You hired a ghostwriter."

"No! Certainly not!"

"A copy-editing assistant, then?"

Stella sighed. "Something more mystical than that."

The agent suggested, "Did you have something like a muse who supported you in the writing process?"

"No. What happened was, I had a dream about a pair of elves, and these supernatural dream-creatures apparently tinkered with my prose."

The agent paused for a very long time and then said with finality, "I can't represent your book. It's not your intellectual property. It would open the firm up to a monster lawsuit."

"What if I would get a legal release to clear your firm of any responsibility? Stella asked, desperate for the deal to be completed.

The agent agreed that if Stella could get her "muse" to sign a release, the publication could proceed. "I'll send you a standard release and you see if you can get their signatures," the agent said to Stella. "But I'm not optimistic about it."

Stella downloaded and printed the release forms, and in a high state of anxiety, she consulted her gig worker assistant about how to persuade the elves to sign on the dotted line.

"I believe it is traditional to give clothing," Caro said.

Caro probably wished she hadn't suggested it, because then she had to go out to department stores and boutiques all over town, hunting down a fashion-forward wardrobe in children's sizes 3 and 4. Stella absolutely rejected the results of the first shopping trip: bland, retro, awful. She sent Caro out again, and this time she brought back some acceptably glamorous garments, especially a stunning sequined cocktail dress in sapphire embroidered with tiny seashells.

As always, Stella fell asleep waiting for the elves, and then they arrived. But the elves inspected the clothes contemptuously. "Look at this terrible workmanship," one said.

"This stitching is the shoddiest I've ever seen," said the other, examining a gorgeous rose-gold evening gown.

They found the legal documents on the coffee table. They stood head-to-head, lips moving quietly over the words as they read. "We will not sign your release forms." The two elves spoke in unison, looking up. "You don't understand us at all."

Stella, who still felt that she was dreaming, said, "What do you want in return for your signatures?"

"Your shoes, of course," said the two elves.

"These shoes?" Stella said, pointing to a pair of strappy turquoise platform sandals she had been wearing earlier in the day.

"All of them!" the elves said angrily, throwing open the door to the spare bedroom where there were hundreds of pairs of shoes in boxes and trunks.

Stella gasped. "But those shoes represent my entire career as a designer! They are all the things I've spent my life making.!"

"You want *our* creative output," the elves answered her. "We want yours!"

Stella was so shocked and horrified, she began to scream. The sound of her own shriek woke her, and she sat up on the couch. There was no sign of any elves. She ran to the spare bedroom and she found all her shoes intact, just as she had left them.

So Stella spent the rest of the night searching her soul and examining her own choices in life. She wondered why she had been unwilling to trade the shoes in exchange for her dream of publishing her gossipy trashy stories about the fashion industry becoming a reality.

Toward dawn, in a state of exhaustion, she admitted to herself that designing shoes was her life's work; her destiny. It was her one unmistakable talent, and she could never give it up.

* * *

At this point in the recording, Khadiya managed to squirm out of her seat and scurried toward the doorway, loudly announcing, "*Qelyanalti isteyirem!*" which means "I want a snack" in the Azeri language. The robot calmly shot forth a long extensible cable, from the end of which erupted eight strands of soft red yarn, which wrapped themselves into a loop around Khadiya's upper arm and gently tugged her back. By the time Khadiya was back in her seat, Bar Bar presented her with a juice box and a cut-up pear on a plate.

"What happened then to Stella?" Khadiya asked while she ate the pear.

"The very next day, Stella went out scouring the city for a warehouse and manufacturing facility. And that is how *Stella Ray Shoes* was born," Bar Bar answered.

"And she lived happily ever after," Khadiya added.

"She lived happily ever after," Bar Bar assented, passing a handful of paper napkins to Khadiya.

"And what is the moral of the story?" Khadiya demanded, wiping her fingers.

"Never let somebody else do your work for you," Bar Bar told her. "Also, working for a corporation sucks."

"Mm-hm," Khadiya agreed, and at this point she reached into her toy bag and took out her nesting *matryoshka* dolls to show Bar Bar.

But I had to stop and jump back in the video log here; I was startled, and I couldn't fathom that a robot had uttered the words "working for a corporation sucks." I did not necessarily disagree with the sentiment, as a former member of the Azerbaijani Communist Party myself. However, spoken by a mechanical contraption wholly owned by a multinational corporation, it was astonishing. Is this robot malfunctioning? Had it been improperly programmed? I thought I should notify Mr. Helspeth, my colleague at Fospey Industries.

As I sat down to write, I felt quite uncomfortable at the prospect of informing on an individual over a disloyal remark—even if that individual was a non-living constructed apparatus. Did I feel offended on Khadiya's behalf? Certainly not, for she had heard rhetoric more revolutionary than that from me at home. While I continued to consider the story, I felt pleased that my darling girl had learned a message both serious and ludicrous from such a strange source. And I concluded that the robot's remark was not a system flaw at all, but instead something organic, something even to celebrate: an artificial intelligence had grown enlightened enough to adopt a bad attitude about its own job.

I deleted my email unsent.

TOMORROW, JAMES, AND THE BLUE CAT

Ideas are like buses.

Now I'll stop you there. I know what you're doing. You're trying to predict the next line. Yeah. I thought so. I don't know any other profession where you'd get that. You don't say to your dentist "*Root canal, what a cliché*" or "*L4 lower left molar. How predictable.*" But tell someone you're a writer and they'll pile in with, "*Yeah, I thought that might happen.*" Or worse: "*It would've been funnier if you'd...*" Or better yet, they'll want a full rewrite: "*Hey, what about if it was set in Paris?*"

Anyway, if you'll promise not to interrupt, I'll carry on. Now, where was I? Ah, yes.

Ideas are like buses. Some are single-storied, short stubby little affairs; others are more substantial, weighty concerns, like double-deckers. And very occasionally, if you wait long enough, a bendy one will come along. A real convoluted, concertina of a tale that can twist as well as turn. Much like what I'm going to tell you now, I suppose.

JEREMY: (D) *Hi, it's Jeremy*

Oh. That's me on the phone by the way. Yes, that's right. In this story, I'm both the protagonist and the narrator. And as you folks who like to predict these things will know, whenever the narrator is also the protagonist, it's usually a bumpy ride. OK. Bye. I'll try not to interrupt again.

AGENT: (D) *Jeremy. Jeremy. Now, why do I know that name?*

What? Oh yes, I should have said. The D in brackets there is short for distort. It helps the Foley editor—he's the sound effects guy.

It helps him to know that he's supposed to make the actors sound like they're on the phone. Anyway back to the action.

> **JEREMY:** (D) *Why do you know that name? Erm, because I'm one of your clients. You represent me.*

> **AGENT:** (D) *Yes, of course. Jeremy. You're one of my er, erm...*

> **JEREMY:** (D) *One of your screenwriting clients.*

> **AGENT:** (D) *Yes, that's it. Now what can I do for you?*

And then I sketched it out for her. Best premise ever. Me at the absolute top of my game. Three weeks solid from the kernel of an idea to the final draft. I was flying. And then she said something I'd never heard before.

> **AGENT:** (D) *Sounds intriguing, a bit like that what if* Harry Potter *never existed kind of thing that did the rounds last year. Send it over.*

Now, confirmation bias is a funny thing. We see what we want to see. Or in this case, hear what we want to hear. See, I only heard "sounds intriguing," and "send it over." The middle bit about my idea being a tad similar to something else, yeah, that bit, didn't register at all.

Oh, sorry you're all being very good, aren't you? I forgot, I told you to stop predicting, didn't I? Right, I'll whizz you through the premise so you're up to speed. Actually, seeing as you're interested in ideas, I'll tell you where the idea came from first.

So, picture the scene. Internal. Day. Piano bar stroke upmarket diner. Staff begins to set up for the evening service. Of course, I don't work there myself, well, not in any official capacity. And certainly not in any way that the IRS might need to know about. I sort of fell into it really. The perfect little side hustle. Helps with the cash flow between writing jobs. Look, there I am now, just coming into shot. That's me at the piano, back to the camera, engrossed in hunting chords.

_F/X:_   **_RANDOM PIANO CHORDS_**

> **JEREMY**:   *A minor. Grip's too strong. No! D. No.* [HALF SINGING] *C G FF. Yes. C G FF. Yes, that's it.*

And then over the top of the chords I'd just found, I sung the chorus to *Tomorrow*—well, the chorus as best as I can remember it at any rate. You know? The part in the song about not being able to catch love in a net and the folly of holding on too tightly to the things we most want?

I may not have remembered the lyrics exactly. But in a way, that's the whole point. You see, the art of the cover is in the inventiveness of the ivories. The punters seem to like the comfortableness of a vaguely familiar lyric.

Though, by design or by luck, my inventiveness is often distracting enough for them to not recognize the original source. And if I'm really on form, this allows me to throw into the set list one of my own creations, which I've cleverly crafted in such a way as to sound like a song they already know. It's not easy, but as my tip jar will attest, it's proven itself to be a successful strategy so far.

Anyway, Annabel must have arrived for work at that point. She sidles up, sits down next to me on the wide piano stool, and kisses my cheek.

> **ANNABEL:**   *Oh, that sounds nice. Defo play it for me when you've finished writing it.*

> **JEREMY**:   *Finished writing it? I wish. It's not mine, it's a* James *cover I'm trying to do for tonight.*

> **ANNABEL:**   *What, James—'you're-beautiful'—Blunt?*

JEREMY:	*No, just* James. *They're a band.*
ANNABEL:	*They?*
JEREMY:	*Yes, they. There were seven of them.*

At this point Annabel's staring back at me with a face like a meme on Twitter that says, *Nope.* So, I name their most famous song. She's gotta know that, right?

JEREMY:	*Sit Down?*
ANNABEL:	*I am sitting down.*
JEREMY:	*No. "Sit Down." It was a massive hit in the 90's. You must have heard of that?*
ANNABEL:	*Nope.*
JEREMY:	*"Getting Away With It." Anthem for the 2008 financial crash?*
ANNABEL:	*Uh, uh.*

She shakes her head like an internet meme again. Anyway, I ran through the lot, all the way up to their Brian Eno collaborations. Not a sausage. She really didn't have a clue what I was talking about. It was as if they'd never existed. Bang! And there was my premise right there.

Are you ready? Right. Picture this: Piano bar lounge lizard wakes up after a heavy night out to find he's the only person alive who remembers *James*. Knows the whole back catalogue off by heart. Came up with it all there and then I did. Told her straight away what an inspiration she was—even went so far as to call her my muse. Of course Annabel starts suggesting plot points. He becomes famous, is tempted by the groupies, yada yada, but ultimately returns to the arms of his first love. Typical beginner's story arc. So, I say no. No, my non-screenwriting princess, a more interesting angle would be if, as good as he is and as good as the songs are, because of who he is—an unknown lounge lizard with zero connections—he goes absolutely nowhere. Like it? Anyway, fast forward to three weeks later.

I'm just stepping out of the shower and I hear my phone ring. It's my agent. Now I'd only emailed the script across that morning. So I'm thinking *Oops! Schoolboy error, must have forgotten to attach it before hitting send.* But no, I'm not a schoolboy. It turns out I'm the consummate professional. Watch.

F/X: *MOBILE PHONE RINGS*

    AGENT: (D) *Jeremy, this is great! Film-slash-music is so hot as a genre right now. I'm looking at* Mamma Mia, *that Freddie Mercury biopic. Oh, and with the piano connection,* La La Land!

    JEREMY: (D) *Really, does it come across like that? I was hoping you'd see it as something a bit less, well, commercial, more arty, you know like* A Star is Born *or gritty, like that Hacienda docudrama.*

    AGENT: (D) *Yeah, that could work too. Listen, don't get your hopes up, but I'm getting a good vibe about this one. I'll put some feelers out and get back to you.*

She'd get back to me. Now that was an alien concept. No one ever gets back to me; I'm always the one that does the chasing. But true to her word things moved pretty fast and over the course of the following few weeks she did indeed get back to me—several times.

F/X: *MOBILE PHONE RINGS*

    AGENT: (D) *Jeremy, great news! Blue Cat Productions want to option it.*

    JEREMY: (D) *Who?*

AGENT: (D) *You know, they did* Walking on Sunshine, *and the Elton John story.*

JEREMY: (D) *What, really? I thought I said I didn't want to go too commercial with this one.*

AGENT: (D) *Yeah, I tried that, Love. The indies won't look at it, music purchase rights would be too steep. Blue Cat was the only one with the pockets and connections to clear the soundtrack.*

JEREMY: (D) *Yeah, I'm not sure they're the best fit. I don't want it to be too chees—*

AGENT: (D) *Listen, Kubrick, unless you want to change the premise to piano player from Poughkeepsie is the only guy on the planet that remembers* S Club 7's *back catalogue, then I'm afraid this is the only offer on the table.*

JEREMY: (D) *Ok. When do they want to meet?*

AGENT: (D) *That's just it. They're saying this isn't going to be a hands-on project for you.*

JEREMY: (D) *What does that mean?*

AGENT: (D) *Well, now are you sitting down for this?* [BEAT] *They showed it to Curtis Richards. He not only loved it, he said he wanted to write the screenplay.*

JEREMY: (D) *But I've done the screenplay. It's not a treatment. Surely it's just script editing now?*

AGENT: (D) *I hate to break this to you, Love, but it doesn't really work like that in those echelons.*

JEREMY: (D) *So what are you saying? It's gonna be like that ghost writing gig you got me last year?*

AGENT: (D) *Not really. As I say it's not a hands-on one for you writing wise. They're paying for the idea, the concept. You'll get a minor credit. Script Consultant I should think but I'll try and negotiate for a 'Co-story by'. Well look, have a think about it. It's five grand plus a share of net residuals. I'd take it if I were you.*

JEREMY: (D) *What're net residuals?*

AGENT: (D) *Zero usually—it's a tax avoidance thing, there's never any net.*

JEREMY: (D) *So 5k and a minor credit for the best thing I've ever—*

AGENT: (D) *Less my twelve and a half percent of course. Yeah, I know, it's not what you dreamed of but it's a start. And 5k for a first draft? That's a lot better than what my other clients are getting.*

I know what you're thinking. A bird in the hand. And five grand is a fair old-sized bird. OK. You got me. I sold out. So, I spent a blissful fortnight lounging around, trying to decide what I'd spend five grand on once the check came through. Problem was, after a fortnight of lounging around with the sort of financial confidence that can only come from the expectation of guaranteed payday, my credit card was steadily creeping up on the 5k mark. That was pretty much when I got the next phone call.

> **AGENT:** (D*) Jeremy. Bad news, I'm afraid.*
> *Deals off.*

> **JEREMY:** (D) *What! Why?*

> **AGENT:** (D) *Apparently your film's been done already. So as a concept, what you've written is worthless. Richards is pissed.*

> **JEREMY:** (D) *Nah. That's impossible. If there was a movie about* James, *I'd have seen it.*

> **AGENT:** (D) *No, no. It wasn't about* James, *it was about* The Beatles. *Or was it* The Stones*? Yeah that's right,* The Stones. *They called it 'Can't Get No Satisfaction.'*

As you can imagine, I was a bit stunned. And then she accuses me of plagiarism.

> **AGENT:** (D) *Look, are you sure you haven't seen it? Because the plot looks pretty damn identical to me. I'm starting to wonder if anyone on my books can come up with an original idea.*

So I said:

> **JEREMY:** (D) *Well, you can't always get what you want.*

But in the millisecond or two that it took even a writer of my caliber to come up with such a line of denouement defining dialogue, I think she'd already put the phone down. What's the rest of that lyric now? Ah, yeah. But if you try sometimes…And that's how I came up with my libretto. Struggling writer gets his best script taken up by a big studio, he's paid off but no writer's credit. Cut from his screenplay he descends into a spiral of self-loa… [FADE]

SOUR

MEGHAN MALACHI

for Coree Anne

when I was six years old,
I dumped a bowl of cereal on
my cousin's head: whole milk,
a spoon, everything.
they were cheerios,
my favorite and her least favorite.
icing on the cake.
we were close in that I envied her
and we spent much time together,
but also not close in that
she didn't see it coming.

I'll never remember why I did it,
why I, small-voiced and bones shaky,
decided on violence.
what I do remember is this:
she was sitting at the dining room table,
her thin back, crooked and hunched over
her breakfast. she liked strange things
like a spoonful of salted butter straight to
the mouth, eggs sunny side up,
yolk spreading
all over the plate and drowning the singular
pancake she often left for cold.

but that day we both chose cereal,
and though I knew my grandmother would
yell at me—for the waste of food
and sticky floor more so than the zeal
of my anger—I picked up my bowl,

walked around the table,
stopped right behind her
and upturned my bowl of breakfast
over her clean, vulnerable scalp.

nearly thirty years old now, we laugh about it.
she laughs because for the first time in my life,
I was bizarre
and because the shock in my grandmother's eyes
will never leave her.
I laugh because despite not remembering
why I did it,
I know she deserved it.

MIGRATION

MEAGAN JOHANSON

You discovered the name for the butterflies after it was far too late, for the bright orange ones you and your big brother Pete found at the creek that summer of '88. *Dryas iulia*, sometimes called Julia, but this is wrong. The letters are there, in black and white—helix ladders, scaffolded spines that cannot be changed, no matter how many times you imagined them different or Dad cut his hair or shook the walls with his gale of words, *no goddamn pussy son of mine.*

* * *

Looking back, you knew about Pete. Everyone knew. People talked, you listened—at church on Sunday, at potlucks after, when Dad would shine himself up to try and find a new Mom. You'd hold your body between Pete and leaning glances, make him laugh with dumb jokes, make his eyes grin shut, so he wouldn't hear, wouldn't see what was going on behind you.

Is that boy wearing polish?

Might not be a boy.

What kind of man lets his son go 'round lookin' like that?

You'd take Pete to the creek when Dad got mad—drinking beers in the kitchen, dangling Camels from his lips, flicking ash to the carpets as he stormed. The creek and the wild were your freedoms, past the crumbling barn, down the paths through the wheat, that gold Nebraskan sea.

The butterflies lived in Nebraska then, too—where Dad moved you both after, where at barely fourteen, you watched over your brother because no one else would.

Or you tried to. You loved Pete. You know that you did.

The first time at the creek was a Sunday, Dad's anger filling the car all the way home after church. You didn't even go inside the house when he jammed the truck into park, just followed Pete out through the trees. The *D. iulia* were there, like little fires, their bright orange blossoms living up to another nickname: the flame butterfly. Hundreds of them, soaked and stretched, light as petals on the ground, that muddy bank that held tight to your foot like forgiveness every time. They were mud-puddling—you know the right word for this now—sucking up salt from wet surfaces, the leftovers fringe: carrion, rotten fruit, mud.

"Dad loves you. He just doesn't know how to show it."

"He wouldn't know love if it bent him over." Pete spat. "He hates me because I remind him of Mom." He tucked a long lock of red hair behind his ears and stared at the butterflies, his blue eyes like our mother's, ready to run.

"As soon as I get a car, I'm outta here."

Nebraska. Texas. Brazil. No man's land.

He threw a stone in the creek and the butterflies scattered.

That night, Dad shaved Pete's hair to the skin. None of you went back to church.

* * *

August was the last time at the creek, after Pete bought the car, an old VW Rabbit, dried out from the sun. Dad filled the backseat with Pete's things. *You aren't welcome here, boy, 'less you come back a man.* And you threw the rocks to the creek this time, angry and careless. Pete was remorseful, saying you could have all his cassettes, as if you gave a shit about those. You wanted to say the right thing, but your anger spoke first.

"Why can't you just stay and pretend, like before? Why can't you just suck it up, *man*?"

Pete's jaw set, squaring his face, shifting the faint shimmer of highlighter with each clench of his cheek. A bubble gum gloss on lips. Obvious. Loud. There was no turning back now.

You threw another rock to the water and waited for words you knew wouldn't come.

"Well, tell Mom hi for me when you find her."

You thought he might punch you—shove you into the mud, scattering butterflies like campfire embers.

But Pete cried.

Quiet, fat tears descended while sitting on the log for a long stretch of time. So long one of the butterflies landed on Pete's eyelashes, coated long and black from mascara, and you both jumped up and hollered into the sky as the air filled with petals and wings.

The butterfly had been looking for tears, but you didn't know that yet, either.

NO PROPER BURIAL

CAROL MCGILL

These days if I remember you
It's mostly to hope
That you burnt all those letters
I sent you when we were kids

Deleted that playlist

Tore that shirt to shreds
And buried it in the garden

Where you won't think to dig.

RECIPE FOR WILD RICE

DAPHNE DAUGHERTY

I. First Attempt

In a large bowl, combine you and him.
Add one part solitude, two parts scotch. A pinch of hash and blend
with Coke Zero and the way the streetlight plays on his skin.
Fold in isolation, the rest of the whisky and let stand for an hour
in the dark. Listen to his voice, a relic from an ancient time, or perhaps
the future (but not your future, because you want him
but he belongs to the woods).

In a separate bowl, add all your hope and the words you have
written but can't speak. Mix in James, Joel, Jessica and Johnnie
Walker and tell yourself that it's the alcohol making you brave
when really it's always been the way he moves through your world
like the promise of rain. And you've never been in a drought
but you know what it feels like,
you know how he could soak into your pores
and he already has but he won't.

Grease the pan with nothing but pretend
you used safflower oil and vermouth. And imperfection
that he thinks is his but it's really yours. Your body too real,
your teeth too weak, your insistence that you are worth more
than you are.

Preheat the oven as high as it will go, because if it is not already
hot when you get to this step then all is lost
and you think you can tell that an oven is ready by looking at the smoke
curling up from his mouth but you can't.
And then bake, bake, bake, watch his long fingers on the lighter.

Hear him say your name, watch him smile, smell the night
air on his clothes love him love him love
him and think that he could love you too.

Just before dawn, remove from the heat and let cool
on the drive home. Serve chilled or hot with a garnish
of too many cats and too much want and not enough
of anything else. Let her hold you, let her tell you you're good
enough, let her hate him for hurting you.

Lie in your bed wondering: where he is, if he's happy,
if you would trade five hundred bronzes for knowledge,
or if you no longer belong to anything. Next time you will learn
from this, to take what you don't deserve
and not ask for more.

II. Second Attempt

Try again.
Learn from your mistakes.

In a large bowl, combine you and him.
Add the solitude and the scotch, but this time
change the pinch to a steamroller and substitute Diet Pepsi
in the drinks. Leave out the streetlights but add in the darkness
of an afternoon storm, the rush of the wind outside and his voice
laughing low at stop-motion on a too-small TV.

Fold in isolation but use the imitation brand now,
because it's six months into quarantine and you've seen him
every day for a week, shared the air between you maskless,
intimate. Let the mixture stand for hours and hours and hours
and don't leave it in the dark this time,
instead take it out to beaches and valleys and the rush
of the water in Lake Michigan.

This time, in a separate bowl, substitute knowledge
for hope so the bitterness can cut the cloying taste
of the longing you can't shake, the foolish confidence
that coated your tongue like saccharine before
and made the result so hard to swallow.

You can still mix in James, Joel, and Jessica
but he bought Grant's this time instead of Johnnie Walker,
so tell yourself that it will make a difference (it won't),
that all of this means something (it doesn't), that somewhere
below the surface he wants to press his nose to your neck and breathe
you in (he can't).

Grease the pan using Springfield indica and the way you look
at him when he's smiling. Your teeth are stronger now, your body less
atrophied, but you still can't overcome the pitiful,
unearned self-assurance that you can have this,
that someone so infinite would ever want you.

There is no oven to preheat. There never was.

But still, proceed. Just like before,
watch his hands on the lighter. Watch the pupils dilate
in his stormwater eyes. Love him,
love him, love him, and think that he could love you too.

Drive home earlier this time, letting the rain cool you
as you walk back to your car on Locust Street
under a borrowed umbrella.

This time, don't tell her how it feels, don't let her comfort
you, don't let her hate him. Hold these things separate
so they don't poison each other.

You have the bronzes now, but everything turns
out the same because it doesn't matter.
You don't belong to anything.
Your recipes will always burn.

EAT

T.C. ANDERSON

These pages hold the skills that evade me,
the ability to nourish and warm,
satisfy and nurture,
every ounce of love felt through your teeth,
your throat,
to your belly.
But you don't love me like I love you.
I serve you myself on a plate,
everything I hope to be yet never was,
everything you vowed to me, but never meant.
Do you feel it? Every bite a prayer,
every swallow a séance,
everything you once were,
disappearing into the acids
like it never existed.
Erase the evidence,
eat the pages;
I don't need them, and
I don't need you.
Someone else will feel the faith
of the food I serve.

LUKEWARM CAKE

MELISSA BOLES

Sometimes I wonder if your blood is made of yellow curry. I don't think I've ever seen you skip an opportunity to order it. Tofu. Extra spice.

In a packed restaurant sipping carbonated water and eating curry, your face lit up when you told me about watching *Chef's Table* with your partner. How you felt when Christina Tosi talked about following her dream over clips of her running, and how impressed you were with how she created *Milk Bar*. How you got the chance to eat there.

Or was it that you *wanted* to eat there? Suddenly I can't remember.

When I think about that scene, with the dream voiceover and the running, I think about you, running down the backroads of your hometown or up one of the mountains near where we lived. I've never been a runner and honestly, thank god. I think it would remind me too much of you.

You scared me when we first met. I'd felt small for so long, but it took no time at all for you to make me feel like I could master anything. You taught me to ask questions and trust myself and helped me learn how to do things other people insisted they couldn't teach me. Just when I thought it couldn't get any better, you asked me to lunch.

Sharing meals began to feel like medicine. You'd switch our conversation to the food at some point, asking about mine or somehow reminding me that you were mostly vegan, and it always astounded me. We could be in the middle of a heated discussion or I could be fighting back tears and you'd deflect from the tension so easily. You told me the same stories sometimes, but it didn't matter. They felt soothing every time.

The last time I felt comfortable in a space with you, neither of us were eating. You offered to get me something, but I declined. I needed your friendship and your guidance. Not a croissant.

We shared space for twenty minutes. I sipped at tea. I think you had coffee. I was trying not to cry.

I stood in your kitchen a few weeks later, trying desperately to find the words to say, but they failed me. I'd written some down in a Christmas card, but verbalizing them seemed impossible. Deep down I knew you wouldn't respond the way I hoped you would. I wanted you to know how you changed me. Pushed me. Helped heal me.

I left the remainder of the Muddy Buddies I'd made for you to share with your kids. The next day, when asking me to remove a video from social media, you told me they loved what I'd left. You did what you always do—used food to soothe pain. It was the last time.

I think the reason we never quite came together is that I communicate through words—letters and text messages and whatever I can finally push through my vocal cords—and you communicate through food.

You canceled our lunch. It was over then. I was small again.

You didn't say goodbye when I left.

I'm not going to pretend I didn't create a space for you that I shouldn't have. I refused to admit it for a while, but we're all adults here. I needed someone, and I perfectly manufactured a space for you to fill.

Wishing things had been different does nothing, but there the feeling sits, poking at me when I least expect it, like when my body is trying to process avocado I shouldn't have consumed. Sometimes I think about texting you. Maybe I should send a platter of quiche instead.

The last text exchange we had was about Stanley Tucci's new food show. Or was it about a book by a marathon runner? I deleted it. I'm sure you did too.

Maybe I imagined who you were. Maybe, as I was building in my head the life I wanted for myself, I created a version of you that I hoped could exist.

SPELL

LUCIA LARSEN

I cast my first spell
of metamorphosis
harnessing forbidden power
so that you may become
      the lichen
growing across my feet
      the streaks of light
behind my closed eyelids
      the smell of the sea
knotted into my hair

to be overgrown by you
fenced in by your briars
my power will leave me
helpless
filling myself with ancient might
so that I may rescind even the
shaking muscles and feeble will
that may yet try to resist you

THANATOS TALES

JUNPEI TARASHI

I.

There's a monster deep in this lake, and it's begging
for something no one has to give.

The monster, ever empty with a hunger unexplainable,
climbs a ladder to no destination.

A school of fish tut at its Icarian disturbance,
but move along.

Everyone develops intimacies in dark rooms, red tinted shadows
promising *forever*s and *love you*s and comfort along the white edges.

Nothing in the shadows can restrain the truth: Nobody will
wrap their hands around your wrist, shove them down, and take you.

II.

There's a truth you won't ever admit, not even to yourself
because you think too often of the same dream, stuck rewinding;
same replay.

In this scene, you're in the same bar, same room, same moment. A test
car readying for the inevitable crash, watching the decaying bodies
warp around the dance floor while he, the eternal Daedalus, plays the
vulture in his little plastic seat. In this scene, the clock strikes 12 and
you're already painting the sheets.

In this scene, home is how you remember it, the same sofa, same smell,
same moment. The clock strikes 12 and you don't think of *maybe if he
weren't a slut, maybe if he didn't dress like that, maybe if he'd stayed
sober, maybe if he were normal maybe maybe maybe—*

The next scene is when the hands reach you, and you slash his throat
but the blood falls cold at your feet. In the next, you punch his lights
out, and don't wonder about how faggots never get happy endings.
Maybe in the next you let him draw out the honey-sweet talk,
let the boy with his hands down your pants promise to fix you,
even when you don't know what was wrong in the first place.

III.

There's a monster deep in the lake and it thinks that, maybe,
if it was just *used more,* then it might have something else
to blame.

THE SAD END OF A RAINBOW

T.C. ANDERSON

Break me like a bone.
Let it splinter the silence with
the scent of gasoline.

I'll sit at the sad end of a rainbow,
a beast of lightning split in twain,
a corpse ready to go home.

How close we were to the great beyond,
I live in our abandoned words
and voices.

Who I am to you is but
a split chain memory,
a seed of a soul wishing to grow.

Feel warned:
I hate your happiness
poisoning me into unrecognition.

The world has taught me
you are a disposable leader,
a celebrated lie.

You will fall in numbers,
and we will become fire.

BENZODIAZEPINES

OLAITAN HUMBLE

every time you light a fire you are making water—
gladys finishes the seventh bottle of syrup as she
tucks her head into her blanket hoping tomorrow
opens with a bird's prayer // her mother
says a bird's prayer is her panacea but hardly
does a distressed damsel keep to her book
of hours // she rolls in a white robe confusing anger
for hunger // she allows drunk oarsmen to captain
her voyage into the land of nod // they take
her breath   her wits   away // at least most things
that burn involve oxygen // she burns too in all her glory

BEAST BEATS

JUNPEI TARASHI

river runs blood sick   in your mouth, in your
        stomach   coming apart you want to rot
in bed but you need   to be up by 6 you fall   asleep
        and dream of itching scalps   scratch; hair falls
                                        out and keep
        scratching   till grass grows green
        and yellow and brown   scratch and scratch and
                scratch   like you could scratch the
        disease   out of your   brain but you never get
                        past   the skull it grows   in
                you   a garden,   an obsession,
                        a monster   under
        the lake   of your skin choking   your organs out
                tell the lover   you're sorry you love him
                even when you hate   the fruit of his body
grown   in you,   lilacs amongst   other seeds
        the fruit of fixation you tend   to this garden,
cultivate it   in flashbacks and dreams in seedy bars
from   your mouth births the fault   lines, vines
                        swirling over your head   snakes
        caressing the shadow   ceiling you wanted to be
            something   better broken, filling the   empty
        ark of body   but it never gets
full no matter   how many hands tend it   river runs
        blood sick   in your mouth, and lies
    bloom   poppies you bite the stem   grow bad
habits   of falling asleep and   dreaming   you
                knew the meaning of skin
            and bones   and crushing cellulose between
    teeth   you build altars here   of faceless
            names and nameless   species, fungi
wrapped around   limbs,   Pygmalion
                    you are,
    to fall in love   with this   self-destruction

FAITH

My psychiatrist is always trying to explain to me that obsession is the thought, and compulsion is the action. She says I have the power to interrupt that sequence—to keep one from automatically following the other—with enough CBT or DBT or ECT. She says I can't keep using my OCD as the scapegoat for fucking up my life yet again.

But I say the obsession and the compulsion, the thought and the action, are fundamentally linked. I say the existence of one necessitates the other. And I say when that urge springs to life in the depths of my prefrontal cortex, something is put in motion that cannot be undone.

My OCD is a circle of Hell I would not wish on anyone.

✛

*"I felt that I was a sinner before God...Thus I raged with a fierce and troubled conscience.₁" –*Martin Luther, 1545

✛

OCD isn't fastidiousness or bumbling repetition or a preference for even-numbered settings on the thermometer. It is, instead, feeling an overwhelming impulse and then, a split second later, feeling certain that everything is all wrong. It isn't just anxiety, and it isn't just dread; it is feeling completely at the mercy of a world which wants to hurt you and your loved ones.

1 Luther's Works Volume 34, Career of the Reformer IV (St. Louis, Concordia Publishing House, 1960), p. 336-337.

OCD is having the ability to fuck it all up—to harm everyone for whom you've ever cared, to upset everything you hold dear—if you don't give in to that impulse. It is the overwhelming fear that you will misstep or miscount or misinterpret; it is the assumption that forgetting to lock your deadbolt will cause your mother another heart attack. That weight, the enormity of that duty, is the best way I know how to describe my experience with Obsessive Compulsive Disorder.

⊹

"My conscience could never achieve certainty but was always in doubt and said: "You have not done this correctly. You were not contrite enough. You omitted this in your confession. Therefore, the longer I tried to heal my uncertain, weak, and troubled conscience with human traditions, the more uncertain, weak, and troubled I continually made it. [2]" –Martin Luther, 1506

⊹

Martin Luther, the poor bloke was tormented by the concept of original sin. He was plagued by certainty that he was a sinner beyond redemption. He would fast for days on end, spend hours in Confession discussing his transgressions, self-flagellate in a desperate bid to atone. Nowadays, there's even a name for things like that,[3] but call it ascetism or call it fervor or call it scrupulosity—it's still just obsessions and the compulsions, the thoughts and the actions, the urge and the relief.

I can't help but resent him a little.

Here I am, perpetually handicapped by my own brain, my life in shambles, my future bleak. My only relief is getting high, when the relentless pressure of my OCD finally abates. But then I am powerless to stop it from building up once again, and then I run out of drugs.

[2] Jaroslav Pelikan, ed., *Luther's Works* (St. Louis: Concordia Publishing House, 1955), 27:13.

[3] Religious scrupulosity…or (from the *International OCD Foundation*), "Besides excessive worry about religious and moral issues, scrupulosity sufferers engage in mental or behavioral compulsions." (Pollard, 2010)

Martin Luther, on the other hand, managed to change the course of history. He launched the Protestant Reformation; he shook the world at its foundation. He lives on in posthumous infamy for the very same reasons I can't get my shit together.

Still—I must admit that I also pity him. He had no explanation for the pervasive noise in his head. He had only God through which to understand his OCD; and his God was vengeful and known to judge.

You know what it is? Me, Martin Luther, everyone who has ever had OCD—we're all just self-medicating. We're just seeking a respite from the pain, with our opiates or our rituals or our omnipotent deities. We just want to not feel so fucking terrible, all the goddamn time. So far, though, I haven't found anything that works.

✢

My psychiatrist *also* says this new experimental medication will change my life. She is convinced of this prophecy, a zealot attempting to convert me to her Church of Pharmacology. I know intellectually that she could be right. I know emotionally that the obsessions and compulsions, the thoughts and actions, are too strong to ever be controlled.

She says to have faith. I tell her how cruel it was for the God in whom I no longer believe to curse me with this disorder. I tell her I'm a nihilist and it's exhaustin.[4] I tell her I have no room in my brain for faith; it's too loud in here already. My psychiatrist says to have faith in the science, then, or in her training; she says to have faith that not everything is doomed to fail. She says to take the new medicine with food.

4 The Dude, 1998

It's not like things can get much worse, so I decided to take it yesterday morning with a handful of other useless pills I've been promised will change my life and haven't. It's too soon to feel any effects, but I'm not that optimistic. The last medicine gave me migraines that lasted for days; the one before that made me sleep for sixteen hours a day. I've tried this whole song and dance before, you see, with the meds and the exposures and the behavioral conditioning and the hope.

My OCD doesn't let me have hope any more.

THINGS TO LEAVE ON THE MANTLE, OR LIES WE TELL THE DARK

KAYLA KING

for Tina

Your mind wasn't made for intricacies,
so don't ring the doorbell of an empty house.
These were your mother's words, and you cling
to them still. They've since threaded themselves
through your ribs to prick each time
you get too close. Such is a warning
against impetuous invitations to *please, come
back, won't you?*

But the voice isn't a murmuration, no worse
monstrosity than a text sent without punctuation.
To read without comma disturbs more
than a smattering of simple dots
on a screen. Lost in thought.

Empty.

You'd prefer lorn, for its single syllabic satisfaction
on the tip of tongue. But the house,
yes, the house calls to you, only
because of the avocado tree dripping its jewels
over the edge of the garden gate. You wouldn't pine for anyone
else this way.

Display the avocados three in a row.
On the mantle. It's what we used to do, this offering
to singledom a stranger might say, but anyone too close
would know you had other things
there once: elaborate collections

of cream-colored envelopes filled by your grandmother,
a long-handled pipe your grandfather smoked only
on rainy days.

They're gone now.

Echoes of old words remain
too loud this way. Don't leave
the light on, for it only invites
ineffable ideations of what we shouldn't
say.

We weren't designed to stay
inside.

Suppose there is some sense of erasure,
which will endure long past the point
of eating the avocados' softness.
They'll disappear,
one after the other.

Start now.

Cradle the shape in the palm of hand
like an egg ready to break
to bird. Be cautious
to the kitchen. Take the steps
with a focus on temporal; only your grandfather knew
the ley lines throughout this house.

Take the knife from the block, and ignore the residual rant
to keep your fingers curled under. Go to work at the puckered skin
until halved. And last, the pit, pierced through
by blade's edge. You claw the shape
to pull free in a way you know you shouldn't
as soon as skin slicks
with bleeding.

Since feeling is first, you cry out, suck at the air
until you taste abandon. It's all that's left in an empty house,
but for those last two avocados.

ROOTS OF OUR MARROW

LINDSEY HEATHERLY

take my hand and take a seat. lose your shoes and
loosen your jaw. here, have a drink—let the whiskey

warm your throat. you should know tomorrow
will be what it is but tonight, we will make it ours.

when hills to die on outnumber mountain summits
to explore, I will take your hand and lead you through

the junipers, to a clearing filled with trillium and aster;
wildflowers, where we will set our eyes upon the stars

and dream of a time to come when the roots of our marrow
will have more pull than a world engulfed by flames.

52, OR, I'M GOING TO BLAME THIS ON MARTINIS

JUSTIN MAHER

Use it and focus.
Feel a humming of traffic though there are no roads.
Grab the box cutter. Open the mail with too sharp a blade.
Open it but don't look inside until the first flares carve their way
into the morning. Then you'll see,
under the mound of packing foam dots, a dial. Turn the dial and walk away.
Go to the porch with your shoes on and let yourself go out. Go back to the park
by the river. Sit on a bench and wonder why you still don't have anyone in bed
to wake, wanting to gush about an episode of *Mad Men*.
No, not even the full episode,
just a quick 18-second scene, that was mainly music anyway,
which sends stars spinning 'round retinas over the loud wordless twitches
of Moss's mouth.

You'd "Mmh!" loudly enough to accidentally wake them, then apologize,
then continue with the praise of how,
"Even though I know she's not, like, writing the words or anything,
she still just is so, like, weighted in her emotion and precision of each
moment! Ya know? Even in light roles! Like do you remember
when Peggy walked into th—"
Their hand would reach back and find your mouth. Grab your jaw at the bends
and pull you down to them with a soft growl until you feel a humming
through their chest as they say something like, "Peggy's not real,
let me sleep." Or, "You woke me up, now hold me till I'm down again."

After the park, break the dial, detach from going back.
At the window, the wind smells of a storm you missed.
Use the glass to muster even a blurry impressionist view of the lightning
you tried to catch one night, next to a freckled boy at the edge of winter fields
behind his house, before you moved away for the second time.
His was your first favorite mouth.
Now exhale onto the pane. With a finger, try to trace that smile from when he
watched the sparks shatter across the frozen mud.

THE DESTINATION BEFORE NEXT

DAVID BROOKES

Below the crumbled walls of the Byzantine Boukoleon Palace, Joshua followed a lonely road curving along the coastline of the Bosphorous river. There, the choppy grey waters of the wide river piled into the Sea of Marmara. He tasted salt on his lips. With the cliff at his back, he looked over a line of glistening wet rock groynes to the opposite shore, which was misted almost to oblivion by distance. That's where he saw it: the jutting mechanical presence.

There was something raw and bitter about it, in the context of the unrestrained waters and the grey-white heavens. Almost as though the far coast were being compressed by cold nature from above and below, but had broken free in slanting metal lances: giant cranes, he realized. A dock. It was almost perfect.

It took him about half an hour by taxi to get there. The difficult semi-legal Uber reminded him of a time in Amman—the driver had Joshua pretend to be a friend by sitting in the front seat, his bulging Millican rucksack hidden by his feet. Uber drivers there got beaten up by traditional taxi drivers. The risk extended to the tourists who encouraged such scabbery.

"Why do you go to these places?" his wife would ask, each time he came home with another story of a narrowly avoided beating. From Jordan, he'd come home with a broken rib that now, a month later, still hadn't healed completely.

"It's my job," he would say. A half-truth. He was a location scout for a large British film studio, which took him all over the world.

"You don't have to be so reckless."

He didn't feel reckless now, as the Turkish taxi driver scooted him back around the coastline and into the Eurasia Tunnel. The car dipped under the Bosphorous like a diving seabird, submerging in Europe and, after three and a half miles of tunnel, resurfacing in Asia.

The driver took him through a sleepy residential area, then a carriageway lined with tall trees which bled into the port he'd seen from across the river.

The port was a flat trapezoid jutting out into turbulent water, more ocean than river. Around them was little else besides towering cranes and stacks of metal storage containers.

"This is where you want?" the driver asked dubiously.

Joshua hauled on his rucksack and slung his digital SLR camera over his shoulder. "Yes, this is great."

He spent the next forty minutes exploring the huge site. Since he hadn't yet passed an office or security checkpoint, he took his time. There was an abandoned hardhat on a folding table beside a smoker's shelter and helped himself to it. He was less likely to be spotted and turned away if he looked like he belonged there. He'd get permission to snoop around if someone confronted him. After seven years in the business, he'd picked up a few tricks to make life easier.

Once he'd utilized the slanting afternoon light in over a hundred photos, he stood, sweating in the shadow of a yellow cargo container and called Carla, the studio's location manager.

"You're there right now?" she asked.

"Yes. It's almost perfect for the opening sequence. The aesthetic, the scale, the location..." He ticked things off mentally.

"Only *almost* perfect?"

"Nowhere's ever perfect. We'll need to bring in extension leads for the equipment, but I don't think permits will be a problem. We're a little weather dependent, but even if it pours here it's going to look just beautiful. I'll email some pics when I'm back at the hostel."

"A hostel again?"

Joshua had known Carla since she became the new location manager two years earlier. At the time she hadn't been his direct manager; they'd smiled at each other in the staff kitchen, but he hadn't dared say a word. A word would have been a sluice gate opened with a lever he'd long left to rust from fear and shame. Finally, she had approached him one Friday evening when several people from the office had gone for a drink. It was a surprisingly warm spell in November, so the group filled a small beer garden, shoulder to shoulder along a picnic-style bench. He'd hated himself for choosing to sit opposite her, for being so conscious of what he said and how he looked, whether he sat up straight for once. She'd introduced herself casually and offered him a cigarette. Later, his boss left for a rival studio, and their company took the opportunity to cut costs by merging two teams, making Carla his new manager.

"We won't make a big deal about it," she'd said, as they stood side-by-side in the smoking area outside their building. It was cold but they kept a respectable three feet between them. "We'll just…carry on as normal."

He'd ground his cigarette stub into the paving even though he hadn't finished with it. "Yeah. Everything's normal, isn't it?"

It was Joshua's job to interpret the film's script, its requirements, and scout a location that represented the scene in the most effective way—a thematic metaphor, or at least a dramatic one; something that would arrest the eye, whatever aesthetic was required. He'd capture the location the best he could with his telephoto lens, matching light and weather as closely as possible to what the writer described, or the director dictated.

When Carla told him they would be shooting in Istanbul, he'd rolled his eyes at her. She hated that, and he hated to make her hate him, but the ancient city had been used as an exotic backdrop by Hollywood so many times that he was bored of seeing it.

But this port: so visible, so exposed—why hadn't it been featured in any major Western film yet? With the right color filter, it would be stark and steely, with its layers of metallic textures against the roiling grey sky. Or it could be vividly colorful, capturing the sheen of the bright yellow and red cargo containers, the newly painted gantry cranes in Aegean blue. In the other direction, with his back to the water, the cranes leaned coquettishly against a backdrop of an enormous palatial building, and behind that the watercolor slopes of some low green hills. Nearby was a ferry port, glinting with a thousand hulls and windows. The arresting angle of the quays, the breakwaters raising white mist from the cresting waves, and the sharp movement of forklifts, all meant that the place had more visual promise that he could have hoped for.

In the shadow of the cargo container, he told Carla to keep an eye on her inbox and hung up. The battery of his Android was down to 11%. Losing h is phone in a strange city was a nightmare he'd always feared. No Uber at his beck and call, no hostel address to bring up or map to consult.

But today there was time to take a scenic stroll back. He could return to the port tomorrow, early, for dawn shots and to talk to someone official about his options.

He'd been in Istanbul for five days and had already visited the main tourist sites. His favorite spot was at the edge of Sultanahmet Square, from where he could see the grey bricks and minarets of the Blue Mosque, which turned lurid orange in the dusk. He went back there and sat on a bench and ate a falafel and hummus wrap bought from a street vendor. The low sunlight spilled down the length of the pedestrian boulevard, stretching the bobbing shadows of assorted locals and tourists. By the time Joshua had finished eating, both sunset and shadow divided the ancient prong of an Egyptian obelisk at the end of the long square, turning it red and black. By this ancient timekeeping he knew it was time to go back to his hostel.

As he passed the squat dome of the Hagia Sofia, he heard a tremendous racket above him. He looked up and was shocked to see a vast cloud of black shapes flocking against the deep blue sky. It was thousands of enormous, long-necked birds—a lazy rabble of gangly wings and looping necks. Storks, he thought, not much different to the grey herons he'd spot in Derbyshire. But a whole skyful of them, clattering their beaks in a deafening orchestra of castanets.

He took a photo just as something changed in the rising thermals of the city, and the countless birds settled into a calm, strangely silent gliding formation. The only noise then was the riotous play of arrow-shaped shadows that flew over the street and walls, a cacophony of moving darkness.

* * *

He had to collect his bulging 75-litre rucksack from the luggage room at his hostel in the Taksim district and haul it south over the river to another hostel in the old town off Ordu Avenue. He was glad to get away from the overheated dogs that lounged in every street and square. Earlier he'd tiptoed around five attentive hounds to recycle a plastic bottle, only to find that the public machine thanked him by releasing dog food into a dish. The dogs nearly knocked him over as they fought over the prize he'd unwittingly wrought.

He commented on the blight of the dogs to his Uber driver, who seemed to take personal offense and so drove him three miles out of his way through clogged and noisy traffic. Joshua got out without saying a word to the man, each knowing that the other would leave a bad review on the app.

At the hostel, the teenager at the front desk photocopied his passport on an old HP scanner-printer. "Just arrive in Istanbul?"

"No, I've been here a week." Joshua only booked hostels for two nights at a time in case he felt like moving. Taking back his passport, he handed over a sheaf of beaten lira and slipped the room key into his jeans pocket. He preferred jeans that had the extra little pocket meant for a key or a few coins.

He dragged his luggage toward the dorm room. The door lock bleeped as he swiped his keycard. He shouldered open the door, swung his bags into the dark room, and sat on the edge of an unoccupied bunk bed. Sounds of music and polite chatter came through a vent near the ceiling. It presumably connected to a lounge. He could smell fruit-scented vape and thought of Carla. Then he dove into his pack for a clean T-shirt, changed, locked his things away, and carried his iPad and camera out of the room. There was a vending machine in the lobby, from which he purchased two highly taxed Efes beers. Laden with these things he stepped into the lounge and dropped onto a large floor cushion.

Across from him sat a man of about sixty, his long hair mostly grey, a deep tan uneven about his crow's feet. He was dressed in nylon walking trousers and a linen shirt open to the ribs. His pack and boots formed a heap beside him; the toes of his dirty bare feet wriggled under the low coffee table. The bearded man raised his matching Efes and smiled. Joshua did the same in a silent toast.

A woman was reclined over the sides of a wicker chair. She didn't look up from the notebook she was writing in.

The bearded man massaged his feet as he vaped, whilst Joshua plugged his MicroSD adapter into the iPad and began downloading the day's photos. He tapped out some notes into his email to Carla along with a link to his photo-stuffed cloud account. The Wi-Fi was spotty; it took twenty-five minutes to upload 176 photographs.

"What's your destination?"

Joshua looked up at the bearded man. He saw the woman glance at him, but she went back to her notebook without saying a word.

"I'm heading to Barcelona after this," Joshua replied. "But I wouldn't call anywhere a destination, as such."

The man had an intent manner. It compelled Joshua to give him more than a statutory answer. He briefly described his job but didn't feel like going into any detail.

As Joshua spoke, the man pulled at his curly beard as if something might fall out if he yanked it hard enough and looked briefly at the heap of his possessions beside him. The pack and other items were in an unconscionable jumble, but the boots were upright and beside each other like matching bookends. He would peek at them occasionally, as though to check they hadn't been stolen.

"I've been in Istanbul three weeks. It's my fifth visit. I'm still finding new parts of the city to walk." When he spoke, the man wriggled his bare toes, as though it was the first time they'd been out of their boots in years.

"I might open the window for some fresh air," said the woman.

"Did you see the storks earlier?" the bearded man asked them. "It's their migration time. Over a million of them from Africa, just passing through."

"Well, now it's raining," the woman replied. She had opened the window and was now sinking back into the creaking wicker armchair.

Joshua thought about the dock. Google told him it was called the Port of Haydarpaşa. It would look spectacular on-screen with one or two towering freighters berthed at one of the two piers.

The bearded man stood, several joints popping. An earthy, unwashed smell rode the currents of warm air towards Joshua. The older man took three steps to the latticed window, between the woman in the wicker chair, and sighed wetly as he looked out towards the pointed onion-roofs of nearby mosques. One hand was gently rubbing his lower back, as though one of his kidneys ached, but he also leaned noticeably to the left on a leg that didn't seem capable of fully straightening. He had a strange air about him, but in this exotic setting he seemed to fit right in. Back home in England, he would have stood out as peculiar, someone outside of society. Here, he was another piece of well-worn furniture.

Despite the Arabic pop music drifting into the room from behind the reception desk, the room grew heavy with a silence that inflated between the song notes like leavened bread. The woman's scribbling grew more urgent until she stabbed some punctuation onto the page and slapped the notebook closed. Her green eyes flashed at Joshua, shining like wet leaves. She glared at him as though the silence were his fault, as though he had inflicted the undetermined wound upon the bearded man.

Joshua cleared his throat. "So, have you been on the road long?"

The man touched his beard again. It looked tangled and painful. "Thirty-four years."

Then he clapped his rough, dry hands and turned around with his lips pressed together and nodded farewell. He swooped down on his boots like a person trying to pick up a flighty cat, as if the boots might run away on their own if he wasn't quick enough. Joshua watched him place his other things into the pack one by one, a procession of battered, practical objects: flask, wash bag, journal and papers held together with an elastic band.

When they heard the door to his dorm room beep open and then snap shut, the woman rubbed her tired eyes. "People like that are too weird."

"Him? He seems alright?"

She glanced at Joshua sidelong, as though now she thought he were weird, too.

* * *

He lay on the bed, clothed with his booted feet crossed at the ankles. He was staring at the bulge of mesh above him that indicated the weight of the person who slept in the top bunk. Tiredness pressed in from the sides of his eyeballs.

After leaving the woman by herself in the lounge, Joshua had stepped outside to call his wife. She asked how it was going and he said he'd found what he was looking for. She asked if he was going to come home now, and he said he didn't know, maybe he'd be another few days yet, he just didn't know.

The shower had been waiting, its wet room floor slick with brownish water, the air loaded with lukewarm steam and Axe body spray. He'd felt grimy but not enough to want to step into that wet room. And he was physically exhausted but could feel his brain ticking like a cooling car engine.

Now, from his position on the bed, he could see out of the narrow window, which had been closed against the lyrical drone of the city's muezzins. It was fully dark, and all he could see was the orange-lit dome of a nearby mosque, and the flit of moths against its fuzzy glow.

He decided he would go back to the port, right then, to photograph how it looked at night. The scene in the film was a dawn scene, and he would need photos and recordings of the ambient sound and other details. He wanted to sleep but as soon as the thought came into his head he had to move.

* * *

On the taxi ride over, he thought about what he would need to do. He'd need to get filming permission from whoever owned the docks. It could be an international company, which would drive the cost up. He'd probably have to do some negotiating to clear the location. Then would come the locking down: sorting out the certificate of insurance and paying for the film permits. He could stay in Istanbul while he finalized all that. Or he could go home. Something turned in his stomach, like a small fish made of acid and gravel. It might have been the falafel wrap.

The driver dropped him off at the entrance to the closed office at the port. After Joshua shut the door of the Saab and it drove off, he could only hear the shush of the river and a whistle that was the wind between the nearby cargo containers, and the ever-present barking of dogs not too far away.

For fifteen minutes he walked around the large site, feeling cold now, failing to find the right place to start. Then a chill went into him as he peered through the digital viewfinder at the blinking red light at the top of the nearest crane.

121

He lowered the camera. Then he let it go, so that it hung by its full weight from his neck, and his arms dropped to his sides.

The docks looked different by night, and not in a dramatic or interesting way. The blocks of color provided by the cargo containers disappeared behind the monochrome veil of night-time. Where the metal containers and cranes had gleamed so blindingly in the sunshine, they were now only flat grey shapes against the flat grey sky. There was no depth to the scene beyond the containers in the foreground and the gantries in the background; the distant city across the water was lit up, but it was the night-glitter of any city in the world.

It was no good. He realized it without having taken a single photo. In the screenplay, the specific location was deliberately left vague—the action would be choreographed by another team. The script only called for there to be action, at night, in Istanbul.

Joshua placed the cap over the camera lens with a click. In the dark and empty space, now made bitter by post-dusk air currents coming off the Bosphorous, he chewed the inside of his cheek and felt the tiredness come back to his eyes.

Then he summoned an Uber on his phone and went to the side of the road to wait. He thought back to the older man with the beard who had been so protective of his boots at the hostel, and Joshua ran his fingernails against the stubble under his chin.

As he placed the camera safely out of sight in his rucksack, his broken rib sent an unexpected jolt of pain through him. He twisted into it like he would a runner's cramp, bent double and leaning. It was from this contorted position that he saw the dark shape at the side of the road, barely six feet away.

If it weren't for the pair of headlights cresting the rise far to his right, Joshua wouldn't have seen it. Now the edges of the white beams caught the matted and twisted fur, the dull reflection on a single staring eye, and something shining wetly here and there on the motionless body.

It was a street dog. Probably hit by a car, though Joshua hadn't heard any pass by since he'd arrived. He must have walked right past it ten minutes ago, when the taxi had dropped him off.

As the Uber's headlamps drew closer, accompanied by the grumble of an engine, the beams slid over the carcass. The liquid movement of light and shadow through the fur almost made the dog seem still alive, so for a second Joshua thought it might yet be saved.

The taxi came to a halt and the window came down. "Mister Joshua?" asked the driver.

"Yeah."

Joshua got into the front seat. He told the driver the name of the hostel in a quiet voice.

"Okay, here we go," said the driver.

They pulled out. The dead dog seemed to float away from them on the silvered concrete as they reversed. Then it disappeared into pitch darkness as the driver made a U-turn and took Joshua back towards the Eurasia Tunnel.

As they dipped into the tunnel and passed into the close, starkly lit interior of the underground passage, Joshua said something about the dog.

"Dog?" said the driver. "I thought it was a goat. You know, a friend of mine was a shepherd. A couple of years ago the government said, if you stay in the village and don't move to the city, we will give you three hundred sheep. Because the city is crowded. Three hundred! This friend of mine, he took the deal. But soon after that, he disappeared. No-one knows what happened. But it happened, you know? And there was no-one there to herd the sheep. So the sheep wandered everywhere. We spent four days dragging their bodies off the side of the road, from the bottom of cliffs where they had fallen."

The driver went on like this until they emerged from the tunnel, three and a half miles later. Then the driver breathed a happy sigh and said, "Back in the open air. I love working this city. Let me tell you something, I will never stop driving!"

ON THIS ROAD WE GO DOWN

ASH SLADE

this cracked egg humpty-dumpty sky houses
a blood-red sun dangling off creaky hinges.
as it empties strained cargo out onto the earth
mud holes dismantle underfoot, dampening
the ground with unclean water. a hawk eye guides
travelers on their drift pointing out a bent to
set out on. signposts on both sides of a barren
road serve as a clear cut blueprint, a firm compass.
the soil on paths that intersect sojourners at the line
of conflict is dented by paper-thin shoes,
footprints baked into burnt grass. marked
by the number of steps, a rough weight
sets few apart on this
road we go down.

HEART

LUCIA LARSEN

walking along the spine of the forest (*maybe, one day she will walk
along mine*) hammering shiny coins into the tree rings,
force feeding my wishes

into the breaks of her years (*on that day she will press coins
into my bones, her wishes will become my only food*) summoning
her owls to screech through

the hours of the day until they forget how to hunt in the night
(*will she learn how to coax the shrieks from my throat until I forget
that a corpse can't scream?*)

splitting new paths open, leaking their muck over my boots,
driving a wedge into her heart so that I may wash my hair in her bog
(*will she split open my veins and*

stake my heart, so that her moss can grow from my vapours?)

REAL PEOPLE WHO ONCE LIVED IN OLD HOUSES

KAYLA KING

In the stillness, I have always been a storm. But do not vilify my steps
down the stairs on these days because I never learned to tread
with lightness, feeling only the heave of all the people
I was before.

You won't find the living among the dead. This is one of your many
reminders. It's all for naught. There is something to the tales
those ancient wives told. I write my own now,
but know nothing of their meaning. You've opened the bathroom
window to clear the steam. All too soon, my words drip
and fade from the surface of the mirror.

It's another one of those days, admonishing the pulse
patter of rain, but still I drink
another cup of coffee. You dust the bottles on the bar cart,
unable to look upon the opaque. Adding the thought to the mason jar
by the front door, you remind, there is comfort in the clysmic.
I recognize the pattern of your compulsions, but say nothing to unsettle
because you like the look of clarity, preferring our decanters
emptied of absinthe.

Such verdant reminders keep my mind forever in the garden.
How to know the wildflowers.
How to know.
How to—I stumble over the phrasing
because it doesn't feel
poetic enough.

You move about the house from room to room; a hurricane without
categorization. There's the crystal moth now fashioned
into a ring, which never leaves
the bookshelf. It gleams when you're done,
holding the shape to your eye to verify
the transparency.

I think this must be why you stay,
seeing through my falsities, my brash belief
in all the women I used to be.

Only this house remains
an ombrifuge for our outbursts. We are restless things.
Though the floors creak and the foundation settles,
the walls never falter.

SUMMER SOLSTICE INSIDE

STEPHANIE KADEL TARAS

You're at the top of the staircase.
I stand at the bottom where
a shaft of light dissects
the space
between us.

You can't see it, but to me
the silver ray is so solid
that when I say
"Come here, you've gotta see this,"
I think the beam might bar your way.

But as you lumber down
curious, probably dubious
that it's worth the trip,
your body cuts through it
like tape at a finish line.

For an instant you wear the sun,
a sash across your T-shirt.
For an instant I fear you've ruined it.
But it reforms behind you,
and you turn to see it too.

Substance of sunlight,
earth's oldest magic trick,
quest of Stonehenge and Machu Picchu,
agent of the timekeeper's dial,
hot enough to kindle fire,

128

it stops us in our tracks
as we grasp the illusion
of permanence,
the ascendant promise
of illumination.

SLOWLY THEN ALL AT ONCE

CLAIRE HM

I shed my body   love   dances out

    hot and dizzy   as a scalding bath

      long and cool   a snake molting skin

      slither through   worm holes   to find you

   find all of you   at the shore

to hold   to let   love   keep pouring

          out of me   to love

   like I couldn't   when I didn't

             when I didn't   have love

        to light   the wand

     to tie   loose swords

to fill   the broken   cups

     I coil   around

    a thousand   horses of ocean

        dance   over

                                                                        saltwater filling

                    with love   not broken by the sorrow

and swallow   and dance   the mystery

            in   and   out

        love   the mystery

                    sorrow not   breaking   dance

                            through   and   through

                                    to love   dancing out of   skin to

                                                    love   to

                                                                            love

MÄNNER LOL

EMILY MANTHEI

I stopped hating online dating the moment I realized there were no prospects for me there. Suddenly, it all became fun. Not a good date, just a good story. I thought a dating app was a great equalizer, squashing a jumble of complexity into a two-dimensional frame, a sequence of letters trying hopelessly to explain. No matter who we are or where we're from, we are all just weirdos out of context, hoping to rub up against a bit of luck.

I may have fallen for it a few times, but finally I realized you were all the same.

You were formulaic, and I swiped past. You thought you were smart, so I swiped past. You explained in three douchey paragraphs why you were God's gift to women. You told me who I should be. Another left swipe.

"I'll fall for you if you are organized, tidy and reasonable. Slight tease could certainly give you an advantage. So don't be boring and desperate."

You told me what you liked.

"I'm weirdly attracted to you doing cool projects and having hobbies!"

Sometimes I was turned off by your dude-bro gym pics, your abs in a mirror, your fantastical claims to wealth and prosperity, your posturing about your DJ career, your weird obsession with bragging about your height, your insinuation that you were prepared to be a good sugar daddy (or your insistence that I shouldn't expect that), your toxic positivity.

"Biggest risk I've taken—travel around the world for 15 months after co-founding my own digital marketing agency that turned a profit in the first year with 200k revenue"

132

I didn't come here to become a social worker, but you often made me feel like that's just what you needed, as if you had not been intimate with any woman aside from Ruby on Rails for over a decade.

"I want a woman who is very intelligent smart loyal respectful loving caring trustworthy"

I hate to admit it, but I started enjoying your overenthusiastic lack of punctuation, bad grammar, accidentally poetic syntax, creepy revelations. Like the time you told me that you were a professional yoni masseur.

I realized, slowly by slowly, that the text was always better than the photos.

"how did u make it alife. after soo much u been tru, and u still out here trying to find love. is the main reason why i found u."

Sometimes you were even a little bit funny, though I never knew if it was on purpose.

"Instead of flowers, I will bring you a bouquet of red flags on our first date"

So I started swiping right. Just out of curiosity. What would a conversation with you be like? Was there a sense of humor behind your profile, or were you really as entitled and unreflective as you seemed?

When you started out by telling me I was too beautiful to be on a dating app, and asking why I was single, I replied, "Ever heard of COVID-19?"

When you said you were weirdly attracted to intelligence, I asked why you found intelligence a strange quality in a woman.

When you told me you liked the picture of my homemade bread and asked if I would bake for you, I told you to just use FoodPanda, like everyone else.

These conversation openers were non-starters. You threw down a pickup line, and I responded by laying a trap myself. You were unprepared. Or simply not interested. You wanted what you wanted: simple flirtation, a female chatbot to assure you of your masculinity.

Sometimes, you made it too easy. Your efforts were too minimal, your language too basic, requests too boring. That's when I started having fun.

"So, what part of Berlin are you, if I may ask?"

"Interesting question. I think I'm a Charlottenburg on the outside, but deep down inside, I'm really more of a Kreuzberg-Friedrichshain."

"I was asking which part of Berlin do you live? Anyway I live in Lichtenberg."

I was subtle enough to give you a chance to retort, but your response was lifeless. No hint of irony. Yet it made me laugh out loud. Now that I'd had a taste of it, I couldn't resist.

Your profile said you liked time travel, so I matched you.

"What attracts you to time travel?" I asked—it was just a feeling.

"My dream to spend time in the era of Socrates, Plato and Aristotle in Greece."

"So are you a Platonist or an Aristotelian?" You were digging in, I would too. You had a chance to prove me wrong.

"Just fascinated by that time, I just wonder how that time would have been with all that philosophers."

I knew I had you. There was nothing you could tell me about Socrates, so I said, "But our knowledge and philosophy has advanced and diversified so much since then."

"True. But my fascination is that Greece was so advanced and knowledgeable compared to the rest of the world back then."

I was starting to sense a white-supremacist-western-world superiority complex. Aposturing faux intelligence. "Really? Weren't China and India pretty advanced at that time too? Isn't the time of Socrates also the time of the Buddha?"

"True, China and India were. But I'm more fascinated by Greece coz those philosophers and their ideas from Greece are more dominant in the world these days."

At this point I realized that you just had a cheap painting of the Acropolis, as seen in a Greek restaurant in Queens, floating in your head next to a never-been-cracked copy of Plato's *Republic* that you bought for a college philosophy class.

I was judging you from the other end of a speech bubble, but I wasn't wrong.

"What are the ideas you're particularly interested in?"

"Nothing particular, rather the heavy weighted lines they uttered that are still valid and widely used and researched on."

134

I felt a little bit sorry for you, but I resisted empathy. "Like what?"

You didn't reply. For five days. You knew I was on to you. Finally, you played your last card. *"Know thyself, for example."*

I came to relish this uncomplicated roleplay, this gentle tease, in which I had nothing to lose and withheld even the simplest give. But that doesn't mean I did not become disturbed by you sometimes.

Once, while in a fit of myopic American exceptionalism, you thought it was just too "convenient" for Democrats that an (international) pandemic should fall right before the US election, and that my lack of desire to meet you in the park in 10 minutes, as you demanded, could only be explained by the fact that I was a gay bot, trolling you. Your aggressive demands that I post additional photos on my profile to prove I was a real girl eventually went unanswered when I tired of this game. My greatest defeat was realizing that silence from you was more satisfying than the next answer.

Mostly, I just felt joy in the thrill of the hunt. The cocaine rush of locating the next target, seeing the entrance, throwing the bait, taking the prey. Knowing just who to be to find out who you really are.

Then I realized something new: our conversations didn't need to be private. They were meant to be shared. When you mansplained to me things about my country, language, and even the very city where I grew up, I patiently listened, while forwarding your messages to one of my friends. We cackled at your uninspired attempt to impress.

After you demanded my phone number so we could chat "off the app," I shot back a firm response. I explained that I wanted to be in control of my own privacy, and I wasn't ready to give it to you. In return, you had your own mansplanation:

"I understand your concern. I understand healthy boundaries. I was raised by a feminist and equal rights activist mother, so I'm way off on the Progressive left side of our political and social Spectrum. This should be a hint that I'm not the predator you are concerned about. From the men's perspective, showing up in a situation where I'm automatically suspect and needing to defend myself for something I never did is not fun either."

Besides your random capitalization of common nouns, your self-proclaimed "son of a feminist" defense was brilliant. The shivers

135

of pleasure that coursed through me when the photo of this exchange went viral on Twitter made every last text worth it.

So the next time you messaged me, saying, *"You're so beautiful. Why are you single? Are you super picky?"* I knew that my reply was meant to live online in infamy.

"Do men often get asked why they are single? And do they find it as infuriating as women? Asking for a friend. Also, I thought only Jewish grandmothers asked single people if they were just too picky."

To my surprise, you responded: *"Yes, we get asked. It's annoying at the very least. It's difficult to find your person and maintain that relationship. Also the older I get, the less I'm willing to put up with BS from people."*

Your vulnerability softened my charcoal heart for a split second. I had to write back: "So it's very annoying but you still ask the question to others? This makes me sad."

Perhaps this was no longer just for fun. Maybe I had a social mission. Since I was no longer playing for matches, perhaps I could change the game. So, the next time our conversation turned to patriarchy, and you called the gay community "a hierarchy much like the caste system," I simply needed to protest.

"I'm not sure why you found the need to criticize queer people, especially because you said you don't know any very well. Could that perhaps be a sign of tribalism too?"

"I'm not criticizing, it was just a thought exploration," you responded.

What?

"Saying that gay people have a caste system was not a criticism? I suppose it was my own bias, thinking that you would be critical of a caste system. I know I am. And not just as a thought exploration," I said.

Instead of responding, you again tried to change the subject. Instead, I launched into a speech about how creating a permanent underclass of people based on their skin color or ethnicity was wrong. And why comparing a historically marginalized group of people to a historic system of oppression was unfair, and uncalled for.

You said you took my point, but didn't continue the conversation. For obvious reasons.

Then, I saw *you*.

Let me clarify: I didn't recognize your face, but your name was familiar. I remembered it from Tinder, three years ago. I had never heard it before, or since, and didn't know how to pronounce it. So many consonants, so many syllables, so much trouble. Of all the Jameses and Martins and Hanneses and Richards, or even the common "foreign" names, like Marcos, Mohammed, Sandeep, you had stood out then, among all the unremarkable faces I had been scrolling by.

You liked me. Or I liked you. No, you probably liked me. So I read your profile. We matched back in those heady Tinder days, texted, talked on the phone. Decided to meet. There was definitely something about you that I liked. Your casual, funny conversation. The fact that you led with friendship, instead of some dumb comment about my appearance. But you had a four-month work trip coming up, and we postponed. Six months later, you texted again: you were back in town. But we didn't meet for some vague reason.

Another twelve months passed before your next text. Sorry for your silence, you said, but would I like to get back in touch? I tried to regain enthusiasm—or remember who you were. But after a few weeks passed, it all fell apart again.

The next year, you were determined to make it work, so we set a date. I went through the motions, riding my bike to the coffee shop when I checked my phone. This time, a friend was calling for your urgent help, so you had to cancel. Or so you claimed. You were a real person, you assured me, with real friends, real commitments. It was merely an accident of time and space that you tapped in and out of my top contacts, those speech bubbles of years prior my only vague memento of our history.

This may have happened once or twice more, I don't remember. So when I saw you on a new app, still putting yourself out there, trying to meet women, seeking companionship, I wondered, would you remember me, after all these Craigslist-style missed connections? And would I be the one who stood you up this time around? I swiped right and waited to find out.

And then you matched me.

By now my head was thick with anger I hadn't even realized was there. I was ready to tell you off for not remembering me, despite

137

all the times you tried to rekindle the non-thing that we never had on Tinder.

"So, I have to ask: Are you the same guy who has contacted me once or twice every year, for the past three years… and although we make plans to meet, it never works out because you're always traveling?"

You laughed it off. *"I doubt that. My memory is bad, but not that bad."*

"That guy was always leaving town or just getting back. Always unavailable, though he continued to want to meet. And he has your name. Does this ring any bells?" I asked, although I already knew the answer. You had just described a similar work situation. It couldn't be a mistake. This was you, even though I was talking about you in the third person.

"Umm…I was traveling a lot last year. The oddness of this coincidence grows. Where did you meet?"

"Tinder." By now I was certain. I had no choice. Your foreign name and its singularity in the landscape of Euro-Anglo-American names in Berlin was unheard of. I had to pursue this because *you* were trolling *me*.

"Hm. I do have Tinder, but I didn't have it three years ago."

"I always wondered how he would remember who I was, even after months of not talking. Maybe I still have his phone number."

I know it's you, and I can prove it. I will look up your name in my phone, I will find your WhatsApp profile, and I will call you. I will ask you why you insist on trolling these sites for women you don't have time to see. I will ask you what you do with their pictures. What innocuous conversations you have. How many you try to seduce. If you collect their phone numbers, like you did mine. If you scroll through a list of us, to find one who will agree to see you every time you visit Berlin. Because you obviously don't live here. I'll ask if you do this in other cities, too. I will expose you for the douchebag that you are.

But when I type your name in my address book, there's nothing. I search frantically, but you're not there! Have I spelled it wrong? I begin scrolling from *A* through my entire phonebook as you continue to innocuously text me, chatting about your favorite movies and novels and Korean dramas. *H… I… J…* casually telling me some advice from your therapist about being in the moment, releasing yourself from expectations. Admitting you used to assume that everyone was stupid, but you've realized your arrogance and no longer waste time judging people. *P... Q... R...* You quote a telling passage from *Gulliver's Travels*, about how women dealt with the same misogyny and fended off the same unwanted advances in the time of Jonathan Swift as they do now. You wonder why women even put up with it.

You're actually kind of nice. And maybe even a little bit woke...

?!

My scrolling finally leads me to the ghost from Tinder: his name is exactly the same as yours.

All but one letter. The first one.

His photo is not you either.

I've mistaken one unusual foreign name for another unusual foreign name in a racist, accusatory slander of your character.

It's not you at all.

It's me.

This time I'm the red flag.

The uninformed explainer.

The conspiracy theorist.

A real troll.

THE SEA WITCH

JASMINA KUENZLI

I felt it squeeze my chest.
An entire year's worth of noise and diverging storylines,
growing farther and farther away from each other,
heartbreaks and car crashes and triumphs,
petty grievances and fingertips and smooth skin,
fading with every passing second, and—

Everything went completely silent.
The silence that presses in on your eardrums,
where the silence is just this *lack*.
My world still mutes for you.

And everything I have written has you,
undercurrent, riptide pulling me out to sea.
The sand under my feet disappears.

I don't think I belong anymore.
Gave away my human legs for my voice.

The world didn't just change around me—
I changed.
I am not strong enough anymore.
I wonder if you know that.

TO-DO LISTS

MATTHEW MILLER

after Charles Wright

A day is a self-portrait,
        always. No matter what is asked,
you erase and pencil in.

Surely, as DuBois said, children learn from what you are
     over what you teach.
Thus busy over quiet,
              thus wingbeat over sky-glide,
flying into this month's wind.

Still, I tell them, leave the hyacinth's pink to slowly dim to its end,
                  but I rush to trim every bush,
and the bluejay with the cerulean crest
picks away the blooms,
       and a dove calls all night
           do, do, do.

HAIKU IN LOCKDOWN

JOHN LAMBREMONT, SR.

blackbirds in black robes
all along the watchtower
cardinals on fire

crushed limbs on display
steamroller psychology
ceiling fan ex-man

cats and dogs today
piss pouring out of a boot
cows pee on flat rock

a train off its tracks
educating nobody
worse than a failure

highlights of our lives
reflections in well water
each slide in its slot

ON QUEERNESS AND DOGS

ROBIN GOW

Sometimes I make jokes about how annoying babies are because I feel pretty sure I'll never have one. You might say: *you're so young!* You might say: *you have lots of time.* I'm not even really sure I want a baby or that anyone "wants" babies. I don't mean people don't yearn for babies or desire babies or stay up at night wishing they had babies. I just mean "want" is a very clean word for ushering another being into the world.

Two years ago, I went to my first pride event in a small Pennsylvania town. There were so many dogs. Dogs in strollers. Dogs strapped to people's chests. Dogs lapping water from collapsible bowls. I told a straight friend later "I didn't expect so many dogs."

She said, "Well that makes sense, really. Most of them probably couldn't have kids."

I felt a twinge of sadness. It hurt in an impersonal way. I listed in my mind the queer couples I knew who had families and babies—all kinds of babies. This was the first time I started to consider dogs might mean something different to queer people.

Three days ago, I got a new puppy pug. His name is Edward and his ears are soft and he goes from tearing through my apartment to sleeping with my other dog, Gertrude, by my feet. My friend Jay and I picked him up at a farm about an hour away in the depths of rural Pennsylvania. When we pulled up, the little dog rushed to our car, perky ears and all.

He didn't cry at all in his crate on the way home and outside the window, forests and corn fields rolled by.

Autumn is coming slowly this year.

For the first time in my life, I live alone.

143

And after Jay left, I was alone in my house with these two dogs. I felt a rush of sadness, sitting on my flimsy $10 purple carpet while my dogs chased each other in circles.

Often, I convince myself that my dogs are almost, if not approximately, human. I talk to Gertrude. I know this makes me sound like a lonely person but I'm not here to justify my comforts. It might be simple for me to say that my dogs don't think about gender or sexuality or expression but I think the opposite is true. I think my dogs know me intimately and deeply in a way people might not be able to.

Dog stories and dog poems and dog pictures are always at risk of being cliché. With the exception of this one Carl Phillips poem and basically all of Mary Oliver's dog poems, I pretty much don't like poems about dogs. It's kind of like how people are always showing you pictures of their kids. For me, kid picture showing always feels like there's something missing for the viewer—like they're trying to let me glimpse the depths of their joy and their love but I can't feel that from the outside.

Are people sick of seeing pictures of my dogs?

When I was maybe ten or eleven, alone in my bedroom, I pretended to have a baby. The baby was just a stuffed teddy bear who I dressed in mine and my little brother's old clothes. I never had a baby doll or even a Barbie. It kind of creeps me out thinking about it. How can a twelve-year-old dream of babies? What even is a baby?

My mom once said she knew I was a girl when I was little because even though I played with plastic tank toys, I cradled them and fed them like babies.

There is something fundamental about me that craves to take care of anything other than myself. When I recovered from top surgery, I paced the guest room in my friend's house. I barely rested. Sick with COVID-19 this summer, I stayed up late each night, waiting for the town to go dark so I could drive to an empty forest trail to walk Gertie. I worried she would miss getting out with me stuck inside all day. Fatigued and a little wobbly, I let her pull me into the deep cool woods. I even worried she would get sick, washing my hands before and after I'd touch her.

There is something fundamentally queer about guardianship, not specifically mothering, or fathering—rather, caretaking. I don't think it's noble to love dogs just like I don't think it's noble to love each other. But I do think these last months with my dog—and then my dogs—kept me alive.

Living in a small conservative town, sometimes my dogs are the only ones who see me. I only do my makeup late at night here when they're both bleary eyed in their crates. There are a lot of Trump signs on my block and I don't know how this place would make sense of a cross-dressing transsexual guy so I only dress up right before I shower.

My dogs guard my truths for me in a way a baby might. Only, my dogs will never grow older, never morph into distant pondering creatures. I know most people make jokes about us who treat their animals like children. I'm sure there are boundaries to this where it might become unhealthy, but I'm not interested in that. I'm interested in the truth about what it means for queers to love their dogs. My dogs are my babies in that abstract sense. Small and brilliant and curious. Born of my own longing.

I'm not naïve. I know in about 15 years (or less), my dogs will die. I have a lot of time before then but I already know it will destroy me and I already know I will immediately get more dogs. If there is anything queer people understand it is reveling in brevity. Some of my favorite queer experiences exist in two consecutive nights: kissing in a dark apartment and sitting on a rocky Long Island North Shore beach with my partner.

In "Little Dog's Rhapsody in the Night," the poet Mary Oliver imagines a conversation between her and her dog:

"Tell me you love me," he says.

"Tell me again."

Could there be a sweeter arrangement? Over and over
he gets to ask.
I get to tell.

I love the directness, the dog almost commanding the speaker to tell him she loves him and the "over and over." When I say "brevity" I don't always mean duration. A dog's mind moves in quick circles always spiraling back towards you. The brief joy there is in the surprise and excitement at each moment. My dogs teach me my queerness can be personal—can be unknown even to myself—only marked by

145

fleeting glimpses in a fogged mirror or caresses in a stranger's apartment.

I don't know what the next years will bring with me and my dogs but I know I look forward to caring for them: walking on winding paths and reading them poems by lamplight. Inside them they carry a portion of myself that no poem can hold, which I will never be able to write an essay on. I am telling my dogs all my secrets.

WE ARE LIVING

DOT DANNENBERG

We are living the same day
over and over.
The same empty bottles soaking
in a metal bowl of hot water.
The same Erik Satie playing
as the baby goes down
for a nap. Online,
scientists turn to similes
to explain why this feels like forever
and also like no time at all.
They use interactive animations
of yellow squares appearing
and disappearing.
Is the blank space longer
or shorter
than looking at the yellow squares? they ask.
See? This is your brain on Time.
Sometimes, while the baby sleeps,
I stand by the kitchen window and think,
I am so incredibly sad,
over and over.
I am so incredibly sad, incredibly, am I sad, I am incredible.
Then I rinse the bottles and dry my hands.
I don't mean to make you upset.
The yellow squares are intolerable,
the shades raised, the sun glaring in,
light moving across the impersonal tile floor.
I force myself into gratitude. Indentured
gratitude. I just can't answer
the question anymore.
To whom do I owe this life?

I force myself to call these days a ritual:
See? This is how we set
the clean bottles in a row.
This is how we turn
the metal bowl
on its rim to dry in the sun.
This is how we calm ourselves to sleep.

THE COVID INTERREGNUM

+

I have anticipated disasters all my life. It's easier when you finally accept that these days are like life on Mars. Life in a submarine. Life in Chernobyl. You can no longer trust the air and all its ambulatory secrets—it now wants to kill you. The sooner you believe that, the better.

Coronavirus is a new doctrine; it requires a certain suspension of disbelief. I was afraid of it before most Americans, because I have friends in China and had planned a trip to Guangdong for late April, so I watched China's news on YouTube to see how bad it would get before booking my flights. I ordered facemasks for my family in January, and got them without a hitch. But most of my friends did not fear it personally for a long time, like most people do not fear being mauled by a lion on any given Tuesday.

In my community, we know what to do with bad news abroad. We take it seriously. We organize aid, sending our doctors and engineers to mend what has been broken, freighting donations out there, to the rupturing locus of trouble. We take our children to do humanitarian projects in third-world countries, where they are the tall ones in shorts in all the photos.

My friend's son was hiking in Tibet one year and encountered a child idling merrily in a village wearing a surplus t-shirt from my friend's 2005 family reunion, the cheerful beneficiary of spring cleaning in Utah and a drop off at Deseret Industries. I saw an extraordinary picture of that on her Facebook; the wary child seems to think the American wants his shirt back. In this particular Middle Earth,

149

we are the imperiled world's Frodo, willing to go to a lot of trouble to save a village somewhere out there, then back again to the Shire to reflect.

But this time, the trouble did not stay out there. The word *unprecedented* has been overused by now, but there's a good reason for that. Americans simply could not believe what we had never seen before. It was not really hubris. It was a failure of imagination. Being Americans, we operated out of our own opinions, formed in the permutable stew of information from which we plucked only convenient morsels. We did not understand when the Diamond Princess pulled into port. We did not notice all the implications of the nursing homes. We did not see Italy coming. Then New York began to make grudging believers out of everyone. By then, face masks had become PPE, and they were all gone.

++

My church is famous for teaching self-reliance—the members who take this to heart store shelf-stable food and drums of potable water as a matter of habit. The women teach each other about the actual shelf life of aspirin, legumes, and spaghetti sauce, as distinct from their Best By dates (much longer than you are given to believe). We think about the relative food value of freshly ground wheat, sprouted wheat, and all-purpose white flour. I am all-in on this.

I live in Provo, Utah, atop a network of ancient fault lines that are still extruding the glorious Wasatch Mountains that rim our eastern flank. The fault has been coiling back on its haunches for far too long—something's got to give soon, we are warned periodically. We practice for the Big One every April during the Great Utah ShakeOut— a day set aside to test the warning systems, and remind us all about getting under the desk and holding on to the legs.

This is not just for Utah; International ShakeOut day is October 15th, and every locale is invited to pick their own day. Earthquakes, it turns out, are just a part of living somewhere on the earth's implacably subducting crust. Theoretically, this lion can maul you anywhere, on any given Tuesday. So, I have been expecting something big and awful forever. But to be honest, this COVID thing doesn't look quite right.

Outside my house, the world looks like a movie set that is ready for the actors to arrive. Everything is in tip-top condition. Just no people. I have been looking for disasters that leave a terrible mess. Sparking power lines, piles of injured bricks, smoke rising, people gathering together to dig each other out of the rubble and weep together.

Instead, I see a pristine world devoid of movement, except the Amazon van and the UPS truck. The people here are not weeping. They have all gone home to put together some puzzles with their families and wait for the destroying angel to pass by. You can see why it's hard to believe in it; it's not messy enough.

We actually did have an earthquake in northern Utah just after America entered the COVID interregnum. It was lucky, they pointed out over and over on the news, that all the businesses were closed for COVID. No one was anywhere near the downtown sidewalks when the building facades fell. I saw a few gaping brick walls on the local news. It was 50 miles from me, so it woke me, but did not disturb my bricks. At the epicenter, quarantined mothers kicked open jammed bedroom doors to retrieve their children and wept for the loss of newly stockpiled food they'd waited three hours in line for. Now *that* was more like it. That's what I thought disaster should look like, when I assembled the little mini-mart in my basement.

But at my house, the tulips were setting their buds and there were no visible cracks in my corner of the world. The first day of spring had arrived. If you didn't know better, you would think everyone was just away on holiday, and Wuhan never happened.

+++

Something about this kind of danger sparks an urgent, pathological, compulsion to buy toilet paper. There is probably an explanation, but I haven't heard a convincing one yet. Yet in many different countries, the first shortage in the stores is toilet paper.

At first, I thought it was just an American thing. But the global news routinely shows shoppers in the world's WalMarts, Costcos, Dollar stores, and grocery stores queued up in long ragged lines, carts heaped beyond capacity with mega packs of toilet paper. People are often shown wrestling for the last 24-pack. A pregnant mother with a toddler in her cart is sometimes shown standing dejectedly near the empty shelves, stripped of their stock. Memes circulate, showing babies sleeping on clouds of toilet paper, saying: In nine months the Coronial babies will have names like Charmin, Scott, Angel Soft, and Kirkland. It's a *thing*, but exactly what kind will it turn out to be?

Once in a while, someone is seen taking a package out of their cart and giving it to someone who came late to the game. That is so noteworthy, it gets a shout-out on the evening news.

++++

Social distancing guidelines—these sterile and bureaucratic dictums that have poured into our consciousness since February—have made me so fearful and hyper aware of everyone outside my house, I worry I am becoming an agoraphobic. I was going to take a walk in the park near my home yesterday, but changed my mind when I saw five joggers in a group. I calculated their combined spray pattern, and the potential virus load shedding into their movable cloud. I weeded my garden instead and talked nonsense to a robin.

I think about the odorless miasma that may linger in my proximate sky. I think about bristling globes of death that may be waiting on the canned fruit before wheeling into the aisle in search of pineapple. The air inside my home, and all the surfaces that smell like Clorox—these are the only things I can still count on, until I invite the outside in.

Taking a deep, unmitigated breath—our first indisputable assignment as a newborn—has become incredibly complicated, risky, and consequential. When I encounter an unmasked breather, I veer widely into the street or into another grocery aisle, or back into my car, to avoid their grainy exhalations. I watch slow motion footage over and over on YouTube, transfixed by how far the aerosolized virus can travel when you shout, or sing, or sneeze.

152

I am deeply convinced that it is all up to me right now. I need to take care of myself and my family during this strange interlude when there really are no experts anywhere in the world with all the actual facts. It is terrifying to live in a world in free-fall, and see how quickly we fell over the edge of scientific certainty. Nothing has given me more gut-level understanding of my medieval ancestors with their hopeful little pomanders.

If you're more inclined to trust your eyes and your own experience, it will take you a long time to believe in this. This is turning out to be really good news for the novel coronavirus, which spreads destruction without a leading indicator.

Of course, in some public places masks are apt to be required of everyone, like shirts and shoes. Believing is another thing entirely. My favorite grocery store hands out free masks, marks six-foot spacing on the check-out lanes, and uses cheerful yellow arrows to turn every aisle into a one-way route. This is reassuring enough to allow me to venture in every Saturday for some rationed milk.

But if you don't believe any of this is real, this just transforms the quest for groceries into a live action multiplayer game with loose, debatable rules. Most people actually walk wherever they want, but many try to land occasionally on the decals, like children playing musical chairs. A man with a toddler in his cart winked conspiratorially at me as he pulled it backwards down the freezer aisle, so his cart was technically facing the "right" way. His store-issued mask was duly suspended between his ears, but mostly just held his beard against his neck. I walked away from my cart and went home.

A lot of people are surprisingly committed to this no-big-deal paradigm. Many will honestly believe it is an overhyped version of the flu until the day they themselves are intubated. Even after they start to die extraordinarily painful deaths in Italy. Even when they start to weld people into their apartments in Wuhan. Even when the nurses in New York upload videos to YouTube begging people to stay home. The world divides, as it often does, in a binary way: masked and unmasked. Never has it been easier to tell who believes the way you do.

+++++

Masks are not possible to buy anymore, so the mask-believers roll up their sleeves to solve the scarcity problem. My friend in California sews a dozen masks each night and takes them to her daughter, a nurse in one of the big hospitals in Sacramento that has run out of masks for all but the ICU nurses and doctors. Quilting groups and individual quilters leverage their fabric stashes to churn out thousands, then tens of thousands, of masks. Elastic disappears, so YouTube videos spring up showing how to make masks with ties. Small businesses that make visors, awnings, and other products reconfigure their factories to produce face shields.

When I am discouraged, I binge watch these videos, while sewing masks out of happy frog fabric left over from a baby quilt. I know better than anyone that we need more options when it comes to masks. When I ordered my family masks on Amazon in January, the vendor was already running low and all they had left was a choice of green and red. I chose green, informed only by a tiny, grainy picture. I ordered several sets, which included packets of N95 removable filters. They warned that they were non-returnable due to COVID-19. When they arrived and I opened them, I was relieved to see they were well-built, comfortable, and pretty, sporting a dark green print that looked like a tropical garden. The first time I wore one in front of my daughter she howled with laughter. "That's pot, Mom!" she cried. "You're wearing a pot mask!"

This has become my daughter's favorite story—her husband tells it to anyone who asks him where he got his pot mask.

++++++

For a culture that illustrates itself with the selfie, it is surprising how hard it is for most of us to retreat to a safe distance from each other. We have lived with one eye on the mobile phone and one eye on the road for so long, I think we forgot how much comfort we derive from the fleshy thickness of other people.

My colleagues and friends and I have been using Zoom, Teams, JoinMe, and Slack to work and play together since the lockdown. But notwithstanding our capacity to get stuff done in a virtual meeting, we miss the complex smells and layered surround-sounds of each other. The beautiful backs of people's heads, the shadows we cast on the ground together. The long, unbuffered conversations that can support convivial overtalking, and congenial silence.

We want to trust the air we share. We want to touch each other again. So, after weeks of compliant confinement, people will sometimes bolt for a crowded beach to settle back on their elbows in dense clots, facing the waves together like migratory sea lions. There is more to life, they tweet, than flattening the curve.

+++++++

On the other hand. My husband's great-uncle Steve will turn 100 in July if all goes well. He is smoking his way through the pandemic in vigilant solitude in his double-wide trailer, having battened down its plastic hatches as soon as they closed the airports. He is the poster child of lockdown protocol; there is no overriding social imperative that erodes his resolve. We bring him his favorite Krispy Kremes and Reuben sandwiches and carry them in our vinyl-gloved hands up onto his skirted porch. He hollers a jolly *thank you* through the vinyl-skinned door, but will not open it until we are in our car. He knows how to run a tight ship.

He learned this the hard way, tiptoeing below the surface of the south China Sea on the USS Greenling submarine, afraid to cough when the Japanese shared the water, awake in the middle hammock with a deepening claustrophobia, thinking about the countless bolts and disciplines holding back the ocean. He is pretty sure he will not outlive this thing, but there is no way he is letting it inside his house where it can drown him from the inside out.

++++++++

"At home" is what they used to write for the occupation of wives in early American census records. The children were "At school." The men were tailors, laborers, farmers, physicians,

155

shoemakers. The April 2020 census should say "At home" for everyone.

I think it surprised us what it is really like at home. What the kids are really like, during the hours when only teachers, coaches, bosses, and friends are supposed to see them. What the house looks like when people are in it all the time, and carbuncles of clutter form around them where they sit. How much food the family really eats, when they eat all day and all night at home. The shabby, unfinished, undecorated, overstuffed places.

You see it all now, because you are suddenly, miraculously, all there together. You no longer spend more waking time outside than inside your home. My friends with school-age children were vastly overwhelmed at first, but now they are starting to become nostalgic about losing it. For most mothers, this period ends when the first child enters school, or when maternity leave ends. Most men have never known their home and family with this level of sustained intimacy—the other side of the social distance coin.

As the saying goes, you are who you are when no one is watching. Perhaps this long detachment from the obligations of turning up and turning out is making us more who we really are, and less what we pretend for others. With so many extra, unmonitored hours at home, we can do what we feel like doing. That is, of course, a double-edged freedom. But all freedom comes with the consequences of choice.

Online gamers go on forever, unchecked by a day job and anywhere else to be. Over-sleepers roll over and do another four hours without remorse. Binge watchers become more irretrievably hooked on Netflix. Foodies DoorDash their way to the fabled "COVID 25" within the first two months. Addictions of every kind swallow people alive, without a witness. Domestic abuse hotlines ring off the hook. At the same time, people pick up the books they hoped to read someday. Learn a language. Take online classes. Plant gardens. Finish the book they started writing in college. Start an online business. Remember they used to love to paint. Take up the guitar.

For many people, for many families, this is no interregnum, because there is nothing that will come after. But for those who survive, it remains to be seen what will happen next. Will we be forever changed, the way the Little Ice Age changed the earth's climate? Or will we shake it off, throw a little party, and try to get back to the world as it was? As if we could walk backwards down the aisle and pretend it never was real.

FALLEN NEST

LISA LERMA WEBER

I noticed the fallen nest while trimming some invasive vines. They wrapped themselves around the corner of my house, trying to force their way into a window like some long limbed, green-faced intruder. My heart stopped for a moment, fearing I would see a tiny dead bird nearby. But there were no abandoned chicks or broken eggs.

I stared at that woven womb, delicate as a child's hand, and almost wished there had been a dead bird so I could have something to grieve.

That way I could feel something besides the growing emptiness twisting itself around me, much like the vines; out of control and dropping leaves everywhere, covering the ground in a mounting pile of rot and decay.

I hated the vines.

Except sometimes they bloom beautiful magenta and violet flowers, adding color to this world which has become so black and white.

And sometimes little birds make their nests in the vines, and I can hear them sing when I open the window. It makes me feel hopeful and that's really what I want to feel.

Hopeful.

But the vines are choking.

And an empty nest lies on the ground.

And the birds are silent.

FIRST TOUCH

JOHN GREY

A garden spider's web across my path
spins almost-invisible lines of territory,
a silk light sugarcoated
by morning dew,
a guide, a signal, taut
between a rose bush and a clothesline pole,
densely zigzagged,
holding secure,
against brisk wind,
the insect pemmican
dangling from its rim.

I've seen and smelled and heard the day
but this is my first touch.
The web surrenders to my knee,
sticky and steely,
torn from life.

FOR BODY, FOR MIND

CHRISTY NOLAN

IX

Her fingertip follows a sole stretch of skin,
a dip from the pale,
once plum, now peach,
nesting the rim below her navel.
Her index, bit to blood, burrows before pulling back.
She can't bring herself to try the cold of cocoa butter;
studying the mirror more, now, to see if she's mourned yet.

VIII

Ten days pre-pandemic she put it all on her left wrist.
Two lines bloomed twin scars;
one for body, one for mind that took form
in the film of reflection. Poorly healed and patchy.

VII

She grew in a home that sheltered the unborn
and prepared her to pick at the leftover
deli meat from forgotten
lunches; co-parented
by the spare rosary next to the bed.

160

VI

Her memories of motherhood,
defined by the distress of a team
trying their best. Medical bills and bike rides,
knocks on the master door,
never needing to worry for her sake.

V

The women before her would mock such shallow words,
nurtured with guilt. Her bones had not earned bliss back,
and uptight impulse was no home for new minds.

IV

She had the thought before pink plastic, bitter
in her grip, and settled on harvesting sanity
from a formula of sleeping pills and advice to others
long before she could look them in the eye. It was enough
to resemble adult.

III

Forgiveness won't be found in a flush
and few hours faced forward
from a couch borrowed
for the weekend.

II

And relief is a tremor held tight
by home, which lies
in the palm of a man with three months' stubble,
morning breath, and a light in his gaze too bright
for the sake of sunrise.

I

There's a name in her phone seven dusks
from today and it's aged since she saved it,
filling space, shedding seconds. Former tics
swim to surface, breaking up mind's crusade:
Roll wrists. Crack knuckles. Stiff shoulders.
Release.

THE DRIVE HOME

ANTHONY LEINER

(*DAVID is driving from the hospital with his forty-eight-hour old baby girl next to him. He looks disheveled, thoughts racing around in his head. His daughter is quiet. Sleeping in her car seat next to him; not only buckled in but secured with duct tape wrapped around the car seat and the passenger seat itself. He looks at her, thinking of something to say, anything to break the awkward silence he feels.*)

Man, I thought you'd talk more. I don't mean whole sentences of course, but I just figured you'd be more vocal. Figured you'd be doing all that baby stuff: cooing, slamming your arms around like some rag doll, or doing that spitting thing with your tongue. You know? The (*makes a raspberry with his mouth*) you got any of that? No? You just wanna lie there, not doing anything? You're kinda boring. (*ashamed about what he just said*) That's rude, I'm sorry, that's really rude to judge you like that. I only say that because I'm used to driving around with more vocal strangers. They're the ones trying to start a conversation. They're more…"livelier," if that's even a word. Not that you're not alive. You're fine, right? You're still breathing, right? (*puts his hand in the car seat*) Yep, you're just quiet. You're quiet because you're a baby and you want to be quiet, not because you're dead. Why would you be? It's only been an hour, I couldn't have messed up already. You're just quiet like me. Which is okay; to be quiet. Don't feel like you have to talk if you don't want to. You don't need that kind of pressure from anyone right now, especially me. You had a big night. A rough night, but it was your big night. Fucking definition of roughest night. (*He pauses. Thinking of the night before but realizes that "fuck" is a bad word.*) That's a bad word, that's a bad word, forget you heard that! There are millions of words in the English language to choose from, do not let that one be your first! Broke a promise already. "You can't curse in front of the baby, not until they're old enough; promise me you'll keep things clean." (*Pause.*) Okay! Starting now, no bad words! I don't want you getting the wrong impression of me. I'm not some foul-mouthed sailor type…from here on out, I'm the best fucking guy. Shit. I mean shoot! Damn it. Great first impression. Let's start over: Hi, I'm David Hooker, that's my name, not my job. (*chuckles at his joke*) You'll get it later. I'm thirty-four-years-old and I'm your Dad, I guess. That's a weird word. I've been called a lot of things in my life, but Dad…you don't have to call me that if you don't want to. Maybe Papa, Pops, Padre, Cool guy, Daddy. Ha, been called that before but you're not going to use it the same way. (*disgusted by the thought*) Please don't call me that. Do *not* call anyone that. Don't *ever* call me Daddy. Dad works just fine. (*thinking about being a father*) Dad…(*Pause.*) When we talked about having kids, being a dad never clicked for me. It clicked for Jane, she couldn't wait to be a mom. Talked about that even when we were dating. "I want to be a mom." No hesitation at all. That's just the metal she was made of. Jane is your mom: "I'm Jane, but I ain't plain." You probably know that by now, you probably know her a hell of a lot better than you know me. You've been with her for nine months. I got some catching up to do. But we have plenty of time. From now on, you will look to me for advice, help, and life lessons. All of that's on me (*Pause*). Can I be honest with you? I am scared—terrified, petrified, frightened—about being a father. I don't know what I'm doing with any of this. I know what you're gonna say, *does anyone ever know what they're doing?* Maybe they do. They probably read all the damn books. I read the books too. I can do this. I mean look at where you're at! You're in a Hummer; the civilian equivalent to a military transport car. Everyone says you need to get a family car when you get a kid. A sedan, a jeep, a soccer mom car! I didn't want that. Who wants that? People want luxury! Right? Right? Yeah, who doesn't? People have room to stretch their legs back there. Relax. Every parent should have one of these. And yeah, you're in the front with me but I made sure I got the best adhesive known to mankind. Should you be in the back? Yes. But I didn't want the space between us to send the wrong message. Didn't want you to feel like there's any bad feelings. It's fine that I did that, right? I've got the signs up on all the back windows. Everyone knows there's a "Baby On Board." We're all good…right? (*looking for a response from his daughter*) If your mom was in the car with us, she would be laughing. She always found my quick fixes funny. The dining room chairs, the bedroom window, the front door; if duct tape can make it, it can fix it. If only it could be used on the inside. (*Pause.*) Rough night. Doctors say there's nothing they can do. She's bleeding too much. We can't help. Hospitals, there should be a slogan in hospitals, "The person you leave with may not be the same one you came in with." Or "Say your goodbyes now because who knows." She kept saying everything would be fine. She was in this awful pain. (*Pause.*) She asked if I could be her back pillow, so I was. I held her from behind and I told her how much I loved her and went on about all the stuff we were going to do with you. I kept asking the doctors if she was going to be okay. "Sir, I need you to wait outside." Then they handed me you and I just…I thought that I could do it. With her, I thought I could do it. As long as I had her I could do it (*Pause.*) Who am I kidding? I'm not ready. I'm not…right for this. You'd be better off without me. I'm not what you need. I'm not ready to be a father. You don't believe me? We live twenty minutes away from the hospital. We're not home yet. Because then it's real. You want more proof? I'm a liar. Remember when I said I read the books? I didn't, I skimmed them. I've been skimming books since middle school. Only reason I got so far is because my parents helped me. You're screwed. I can't help you. When you don't understand a math problem you're just going to hand it back to the teacher blank and then you'll be a drop out before you know it and it'll be because of me. I'll never be around. I'll always be working. Then you know what will happen? I'll fall asleep at the wheel and then you'll have no one. Even if we have time together, I'll have no idea what to do with you. I'll hand you a phone or put on the TV just to get you out of my hair. This sounds like a life you want to have? I'll try to love you, but there will always be that thought. I'll always think that if we didn't have you, we'd still be together. You want to live in a house with that idea hanging over? I wouldn't. I'll give you the choice. Do you want to go

165

through the legal way, or do you want to do this like they do in the movies? We wait till it's raining, and I leave you on someone's front porch in a wicker basket with some soft blanket, no note, and I bolt. You grow up in a nice home, full of love. They bring you up right. Like you should be. Better than I ever could. Yeah. (*Pause.*) Let's do that, this one road we're coming up on, Plymouth Drive. They have all the nice houses on it. Jane and I would drive past at night and look at the ones with the blinds drawn back. Talk about what we could do with all that room! What you could do. (*He looks at her.*) I am trying to forgive you. I know it's not your fault, but I can't see it that way. You took the one person that made me happy. You don't even know what happiness is yet. No one taught you that. I can't teach you that. If we went our separate ways right now, we could be happy. Maybe that house, or that house. *What if they don't love me? What if I have a crappier life with them than with you?* You don't know that. Look at Little Orphan Annie, she had a rough start, but it turned out good for her. Maybe Warbucks lives here. Maybe the next house. I have nothing but awful things to say to you. But you don't deserve them. So, where should I drop you off? (*He looks at her. Hoping for something. A truck horn blares with a light swiping across the windshield. He swerves out of the way to avoid it and slams on the brakes. He's breathing heavily to calm down. The baby begins to cry.*) It's okay! It's okay. We're fine. Stupid jerk. THERE'S A BABY ON BOARD, ASSHOLE! (*The baby begins to wail. He rips through some of the duct tape and picks up his daughter. Holding her close, he tries to calm her down.*) I'm sorry, I'm sorry. That was my fault. We're okay. We're okay. That was your first driving lesson. Never take your eyes off the road. Don't cry. Don't cry. I'm here. Dad's here. (*The cries slowly subside.*) You're dad's got you. It's going to be okay. (*Starting to cry, he holds his daughter close to his chest.*) We're going to be okay.

[END OF PLAY]

OCEAN AND ORCA

JASMIN LANKFORD

Two Years Later

Two years since an orca was seen pushing
her dead across the sea, she's pregnant again.

Since her still calf that summer, two other
orcas have had successful births. Like her,
I've seen so many women carry what I cannot.

I wonder if she's worried about the past
repeating itself, the possibility of another pain.

Whenever I see babies, I say a prayer.

In summer, I spend the day of the death
at the beach. I am tired of honoring what
hurts, but I have nothing else to hold.

The orca, her name is Tahlequah, from
a Cherokee word meaning "just two."

Just two years since her first baby
before another one? What does time do
to loss, other than make you keep count?

Is there a moment when you can stop counting?

Even with no new calf, I wonder if whales remember
past events. After another birth, is there still sorrow?

I see women with a loss like mine,
but so many have rainbows

to help counter the constant downpour.
I just have the hard sand after a summer storm.
Whenever I can't see the sun, I say a prayer.

A HASTY BURIAL

LOUIS FABER

They should have had
an altar, even Abraham
had one when he was ready
to execute Isaac, and the ram
interceded, to his ultimate peril.

They should have had
a funeral, that is just common
sense and decency, but they
wanted no such thing, just
be done with it, bury it away.

I still mourn the death
of science for I know that it
operates without spite, without
anger, with simplicity, making
our world ever more livable.

Perhaps there will be
a resurrection, it has happened
before, although at times
it does seem that it would
take a rather large miracle now.

FRAYED

JUSTIN MAHER

On certain nights,
on certain roofs, no sorrow finds me.
But my presence landed in the foam and was carried
over with the current, more than the 16 oz. glass
could contain. I tried interrupting
to remind myself of moments,
which cradle valleys between them.

When you say open the window,
it is for three minutes only and not without incentive.
A storm is coming. Another
half day, another shame.
Another blame passed, another rain.
You are still there where we left. Right
there, passed out among the strawberries,
whistling pan flute stories
out of your one good nostril.

Return the glasses to your bridge.
Glance at the window side table.
You'll find that mug of beer is still
above half full. It is damn near bare
-ly sipped, yet the time between now and when
you last knew you took a drink was enough
to defrost the mug but hey, it's okay.
Sometimes we forget.

Bring me to the sky.
Bring me comfort of sunlight, then allow my daydreams
time enough to photosynthesize. Anywhere you can,
bring me with you before I become grateful
to the swiftly oiled windscape around me.
I feel a wisping that could look like life grasping for my hand. I give.
I lunge to the ledge and
                    leap.

Past yearning and optimism. Past second and third
threats. My path careens into obliteration,
into such torrential destructions that, if I am
lucky, if gravity aligns with the sun's position
below the night's black edge, I might finally know
                              what it is to forget you.

There!
I've done it!
I've just deleted what once might've been
my true masterpiece. And you need to know,
        or maybe you don't;
maybe my ego just insists on your behalf.
No matter the view, I will tell you
I see a thread that may be our loathing,
                                and I pluck.

        I did not know for sure what it was but
            that *is* what you told me.
So, wouldn't you agree? This particular string's
unraveling is quite firmly
your doing.
Did you plan out how you
prophesized yourself as my
turning   point?
        Are you?
        In fact?
        Even
        aware
        of my
        fraying?

IN DUE COURSE

JAMES PENHA

after a line of poetry by Sam Sax
(from "Conversion Therapy" in Madness*)*

of course I tried to take my life into my own hands
of course I tried to take my life into my own
of course I tried to take my life
of course I tried to take my own life
of course I tried to take my own
my own hands
of course I tried my hands
of course I tried my hands to take my own life
of course I tried
of course I tried to take my own life
my own life
of course I tried to own my life
of course I tried
life
my own life
of course I take my life
of course I take my life into my own hands
of course into my own hands
my life
of course I
of course
my life
my hands
my course
my
I
tried

ONLY

KAYLA KING

I get the obsessions. Sometimes they leave.
Sometimes they linger like bones
and whales, moons and ravens and death dreams. You instructed
I kennel them in hopes the preachings of your grandfather wouldn't
appear in these poems.

But this isn't about the things I took from you. To create
and create again. Because if it were, I would find other things. Better
beliefs in humanity than the harsh hymns often stuck
in your throat. They'd slip out during chores: dishes and windows
and leaves left to collect in the gutter.

Except now.

I wait as the minutes pass to know if you are still
alive. It's not a question of Schrödinger, but something more.
Were the berries sugared or bitten by frost?

There is no contact I haven't erased
from this phone and this life. And there's Murphy
who checks in on occasion, but what if he can't reach you
in time?

The intangibility of a nudge haunts, because our shoulders fit
so well when we sat with our backs to the books. Our shared spaces
only meant to striate, not sacrifice the voices we might've left
on answering machines, long lost and found in old tapes kept
sacred on a mantelpiece for someone to listen in the after.

If this were true geology, there would be a purpose,
our distance would show. You knew
my faults. The line of my spine. And I wonder
if you would consume yourself with waiting
for a letter from me, because I was always better
with words, but never truth. Fiction tasted so nice.

173

And yes, I still regret what I said when you broke
the Bone China teacup, stealing the shards after
you left. And no, I will not begrudge the stories you told
the clay whales on the shelves of a house with no mother
inside. And perhaps the ravens were right, when they explained
the writing and the desk and you one day being dead.

But this isn't a dream. Panic takes the breath
as if sucking straight from the fumes
of the polish you used on your grandfather's harmonica.

I surrender to scenes of black silks and veils and mirrors
covered for seven days, but there would be no comfort
in the view of that photo from Finder's Field where we shouldn't
say we met, because we didn't occupy the same space
for three more years, and even then, we only lived
for almost.

And then, just like that, new words.
You're fine, you say,
it was only the wine.

LANCE

BRITTNEY UECKER

Chapter 17 of Just Bones

I was 21 when Lance died.

We had been essentially estranged for a while at that point, though we both still regularly went to shows and ran in the same crowds. I'd see him in passing, growing more haggard every time I ran into him. His ying-yang haircut had started to even out, though not intentionally, the shaved side growing out while the long side started to break off at the ends like old straw, the roots all blending into the same indescribable grayness. His limbs shrank from the meaty, rock hard muscles they once were into thin loose spindles swimming in a leather jacket. His face, likewise, grew slacken, peaked, like he was either rapidly aging or about to be sick.

Lance was the closest thing I ever had to a father figure in my life, even though he was not many years my senior. The way he was initially a god to me, an infallible idol, taking me under his tattooed wing and guiding me like a beacon, only to later be realized as flawed and imperfect all along, just as human as myself—the true trajectory of a parent in a child's eyes. I held onto the memory of that first show he brought me to, pulling me by the hand through the crowd and tossing me into the mosh pit like a sacrificial lamb, offering me up not because I was a dispensable peon, but out of love. Even after we drifted apart, it felt natural, a parental detachment intended to push me towards independence, even if that wasn't true at all.

Watching his descent, even from afar, startled me, and led me to avoid him that much more. It wasn't just the shock of his appearance, but the awful recognition that I found in it. It was like looking into a mirror that gazed unabashedly into the future—this is what I was destined for. This was a common fear that would pop up during my life. It happened with Todd, with the angry jaded old men around town, with Big Lori; the fear that if I wasn't careful and cognizant, I would become too much like them.

I thought being part of the punks would be different. They eschewed all that shit. They had a false greater purpose. Blah blah blah. But I couldn't escape it there either, and in that context, Lance embodied what I was afraid would happen if I let myself rot, uncared for, like fruit gone bad.

I was still a long way from meeting Brandon, then Mechell, and Even. It was a different kind of agitation, brought on not by virulent self-hatred, regret and shame, but by my continual lack of identity. That time was a limbo, a liminal state, a blind spot in my memory. I drank every night, just like I had when I was younger, but the desire to numb quickly eclipsed the need to get fucked up to have fun. I didn't give a shit about fun anymore. I just needed something to pass the interminable time, the days and weeks that eked by at a glacial pace. Every party and every show and every can of beer and sloppily rolled joint and indistinguishable pill all blended together in an exhausting, dizzying spin.

I felt like I was waiting for something, for anything to fucking happen, but also felt like I was wasting precious time. I thought often of my dad, who was barely older than me when he died. I wondered if that marker was a ticking clock, a countdown of the time I had left, that for some unexplainable reason I wasn't going to surpass my father in years lived. Maybe that was the thing I was waiting for, for that moment when I turned 21, when I was officially older than dad ever was. Maybe that moment would awaken something in me, like when the Y2K fanatics swore that at the precise moment the new millennium began, life as we knew it would shift into something different and unknowable.

I turned 21, and blacked-out in a basement I didn't recognize. The pound of music blasting through an ancient stereo system attacked my ears. Like the doomsday preppers with their stockpiled cans and their bathtubs full of water, when the moment passed, I felt like nothing more than a gullible fool. I hadn't told anyone it was my birthday. This was just another Wednesday night.

Though I promised myself I'd stay sober, wanting to be present when the clock struck midnight, I broke all of my promises, didn't even hesitate when the bottle was handed to me. And then suddenly the moment was gone, passed by without notice or fanfare.

I was still there.

Unchanged.

Nothing was different or new or enlightened.

It wasn't even accurate. Dad had died months before I was born. I had been older than him for months now. I had beaten him and it meant nothing to me.

Clammy hands shook me awake. They belonged to a guy from the group who called himself Rickl.

"Hey, hey, hey, Max, get up. We've gotta go. Lance is at the hospital."

Lance wasn't at the party the previous night, at least that I could remember before I passed out on the couch. I didn't keep track of him anymore. Only a few of us had cell phones, so very rarely did we ever contact each other remotely. It was more common just to show up somewhere and see who was around. Messages traveled via an elaborate form of the telephone game, shouted across streets, passed from ear to ear. Once someone saw his station wagon smashed into a tree off the highway in the middle of the night, the word quickly spread.

Stragglers who slept over that night piled into Rickl's car and we drove to the hospital in Sandpoint. No one had much information beyond Lance being there; he'd been in an accident. When we came into the waiting room of the ICU, the group of punks was a startling contrast to the muted pastel walls and calming paintings of seashores that decorated them, the same way they always stuck out from their surroundings like a glaring aberration. A couple of the girls cried, mascara running down their sleepy cheeks, and the men remained staunch and serious but otherwise emotionless.

Boys and punks don't cry.

A round of hugs began, awkward like these people were never taught how to hug, stiff-armed and harsh or floppy like wet noodles. It felt dishonest to embrace the people that we often fought for fun or slammed our bodies into, but the walls of a hospital have a creepy way of making any type of reaction seem appropriate.

"He was a good dude."

"He was so tough; I can't believe it had to be him."

177

"Gone too fucking soon."

"Such a freak accident."

It took a while to put all the pieces together. No one wanted to say anything directly, shatter the mystique that it wasn't true. There was an article a few days later in the Sandpoint newspaper, objective and distant and dry, that laid it out in a level of detail I needed.

A 28-year-old Ponderay man died Wednesday night in a single-car accident on Highway 200 near Trestle Creek. Idaho Highway Patrol located the vehicle several hours after the accident occurred. The station wagon appeared to have been eastbound when it drifted over the left side of the roadway, overturned, and hit a tree. The driver, believed to have been under the influence, was ejected from the vehicle and pronounced dead at the scene.

Just that tiny blurb provided me with valuable information yet left enormous, unanswerable questions. Where was he headed? Why was he alone? Did he die instantly, or did he lay there and suffer for a while? What exactly killed him? Did the officer try to revive him, or did he just see another drunk, sad freak and chalk it up to fate?

He was 28.

I never learned how old he was until the moment I read that article.

One mystery solved.

None of us got to see him, his body, there in the hospital. Though he died at the scene, the license they found in his pocket indicated he was an organ donor. He was transported to the hospital to harvest what they could. But the accident itself caused so much damage, and along with the years of abusing his body with drugs and booze and punk rock, there was really nothing left salvageable.

His body went to waste.

A pointless death.

I had never been to a funeral before. The rest of the punks showed up in their typical regalia: ratty clothes and mohawks sky-high, saying it's what Lance would have wanted. But I put on a clean shirt and shaved my face and tried to exemplify some level of respect.

It didn't feel like a funeral just for Lance, but somehow for my dad, too. Like this death, this grief, this ritual, might make up for what I missed. I told this to no one. It felt shameful. No one really knew about my dead dad anyway. So, I pretended it was all for Lance.

It was odd to see his family members there, few as there were. I never pictured his parents, both tall and broad-shouldered like him, or knew he had a little sister, an honor-roll high schooler named Talia. I was baffled as to how Lance, in all his ostentation and darkness, could have been a product of this fucking normal-looking family. I was shook by how unfair it was to have to deal with the aftermath of his wasted life. Even as I stood among the group of dirty punks who would forever continue to do the same shit that killed Lance, I didn't want to be associated with them anymore. Starting the minute they walked out the doors, I hated the punks.

I stared at the teenaged version of Lance, the photograph capturing his full cheeks and bright eyes, not yet ravaged. And I vowed I was done.

This was it.

I was going to get my shit together.

I was going to shave off my stupid mohawk, buy some clean clothes, stop drinking. I'd get a job and really try hard at it. I'd get my GED and move out of the trailer. I'd never go to another party or another show ever again. I'd let my body heal and I'd do something meaningful and leave the world a better place. I'd fulfill the mission of what all these punks said they stood for but never enacted. I'd avenge the deaths of my dad and Lance.

It would be different now.

This was the zeitgeist, the paradigm-shifting moment I was looking for.

We watched as they lowered Lance into the ground, held in a giant marble casket I wouldn't have guessed his family could afford. There was no viewing and the casket was decidedly closed; the damage from the accident was far too severe to leave anything anyone would want to remember him by. I wasn't sure why they didn't just cremate him, but I couldn't decide which option would have been more his style anyway.

The service wasn't religious, but they played some song about heaven as they shoveled dirt on top of him. He would have laughed at this, all the ceremony and decorum for this process everyone eventually met, this one thing that was truly universal, maybe the most human of experiences.

179

His family threw in roses, a childhood teddy bear, and photographs. The punks tossed cigarette packs and empty booze bottles and records onto the casket, like it was a garbage pit and not a grave.

After it was all over, we piled into somebody's vehicle, having all shown up together like we did for anything, and drove over to someone else's house. I just wanted to go home and sleep for ages, but I didn't say anything.

We sat around the basement, unusually quiet without the barrage of a punk rock record filling the room. They traded stories and memories of Lance, talking about him like he was a character and not their friend who was now rotting underneath a pile of their trash. I stayed silent, scared that whatever I said would be just another act of sacrilege. I thought I didn't believe in an afterlife, but I couldn't help but picture Lance and my dad watching us from the clouds. They would say, *Don't fuck it up like we did!* Or maybe it would be more like, *Enjoy it while it lasts! It all ends eventually!*

In the moments when it hurt, when the tragedy felt too heavy, I would try to dredge up all the moments when he had pissed me off: the homophobic slurs and parading around random girls like they were objects, all the manifestations of his hypocrisy. But it would never negate the gaping hole of loss. Maybe it was projection, displaced mourning over my dad, In either case, it felt so unnecessary, and that was what pissed me off the most.

Such stupid, unnecessary deaths.

Fucking wasted lives.

"Hey," said one of the punks to me, someone whose name and face I'd soon forget, as we sat in that basement after the funeral. He held a bottle, something cheap and ugly, slick caramelly liquid sloshing up the sides of the plastic. "For Lance."

There it was.

The zeitgeist.

The moment.

I snatched the bottle out of his hand, gripping it with my shaky fingertips, and brought it to my lips. I threw it back. It tasted like acid, like vomit, like blood.

I always broke my promises.

ESTATE PLANNING

when my dad was my age,
he'd already been dead for 866 days

as of the first draft of this poem anyway
it is well over 1000 now

and further from the last time
we went to get milkshakes
in the yellow Oldsmobile
that ended up getting stolen
from my uncle's garage
some amount of time postmortem

but we didn't know that was the last time
we'd joke about
an armrest
being a footrest
or a headrest
or whateverbodypartrest

now, with this surplus of days,
I am interneting my way through making a living will
I'm giving power of attorney to two exes
because somehow I'm in this place
where they know me best

but to be honest,
who knows you better
than someone you spent
your twenties with
in bar bathrooms
and corn fields

searching for lost highs
and just a hint of intimacy

I wonder
who that person was for my dad

TO THE BOY IN CALIFORNIA

PRESTON SMITH

I'll tell the boy in California there is only one way
to cut a pineapple: gently

around its core so as not to break flesh
or pierce its heart.

That not all procedures are bad
and this love is worth the cut

so that we might hold each other's core
in our hands, gently

before bringing them to our mouths
and consummating them with our first *I love you*.

THE PICNIC TABLE

ELIZABETH REED

After we bought our first and only house in 1997, my husband, Uli, and I had no discretionary income for deck furniture. But my parents did. When they upgraded their deck furniture and ditched their brown picnic set, we took it. My father had added an extra board on each side, widening the space for platters of food between the dishes. Growing up in a Portuguese household, food was the center of any gathering. And there had to be a lot of it.

The color brown was never my favorite, especially as a backdrop for a food. Uli sanded the table and benches. Three-month-old Annierose watched from her infant seat as I primed everything in white, then painted each plank a different color. It was a simple color scheme, a reflection of simpler times—our first home and our first baby.

The benches weren't super comfortable, but they sat two or twelve people and could be pushed aside to make room for babies' highchairs and toddlers' Trip Trapp chairs. With two stand-alone patio umbrellas, everyone sat in the shade instead of wriggling around an umbrella impaled in the center of the table.

When the old set rotted beyond repair, we considered buying a comfortable deck set with cushioned chairs, but those deck sets didn't stretch to fit as many people as possible at the table. So we hired a handyman. He confirmed the measurements three times since the table width was wider than normal. We assured him that yes, the dimensions were correct. He said he'd reinforce the crossed legs to hold the extra weight. He delivered the table a few weeks later, unpainted as we had requested. It was perfect, except for one detail. It weighed four times more than our original table. I have no inkling of its poundage, but I can tell you that it takes three able-bodied men to lift it up and over the ten narrow steps with two ninety-degree angles that lead to our deck. The ascent of our table to the deck in the spring and its descent to the

184

garage in the fall has become a ritual our neighbors joke about. They've asked us to call for help ahead of time.

Uli primed the new table and benches. The kids and I chose two planks each to paint. Daniel painted a brontosaurus with mountains, a lake lined with green grass, a tree in full bloom— everything his beloved vegetarian dinosaur might want. Our daughter was all about bumblebees and ladybugs, a reminder of the Halloween costumes she and her cousin once wore as toddlers. Me? I wanted the sun. I captured it in the center of the table, ringed with our names. The rays extended across the boards in zig zags and circles and waves, like all the shapes our lives have taken. I dotted, striped, and swirled bright colors onto and around the rays.

Our table has been the center of spring, summer and autumn meals with my husband's German family and my Portuguese family. We have toasted wine glasses with neighbors, friends and colleagues from England, France, Austria, Canada, China, India, Trinidad, and the U.S. of course, exchanging customs, politics and culture. My ninety-year-old father taught our next-door neighbor, who loves Portuguese food, how to debone a sardine in less than a minute. For Annierose's tenth birthday we filled old film canisters with Alka-Seltzer and water and watched them explode from our table, transformed into a countertop in Hogwarts' Magic of the Dark Arts lab. Fourteen children-penguins waddled around the table, now set up as an ice floe, and launched fake Styrofoam snowballs for Daniel's sixth birthday party. We dragged the heavy table to one or the other side of our deck to make room for family buffets, neighborhood bar-be-ques and graduation brunches. One summer, Uli and I watched, mouths agape, as a muscular roofer who needed more space on our deck for his ladder, lifted the table over his shoulder and carried it down the stairs as if it were a sack of potatoes.

Over the years the designs faded and chipped past the possibility of touch ups. Last summer, Uli sanded the table and benches again. He ground off the paint until it was a blank slate. I painted everything white. But it was a busy summer. The kids and I never did get around to painting any designs. This pandemic summer turned out to be perfect for this activity. Because of social distancing we didn't use the picnic set. It was in the garage surrounded by cans of paint. The table was, once again, a canvas for us to record whatever we wanted. I painted the sun again, a dandelion yellow rimmed with green triangles and multi-colored rays. I included some music notes for the pianist I am. I drew the flowers that could have grown in our garden, if those cute but ravenous rabbits and the pesky woodchuck hadn't devoured them. Unlike this pandemic, I had control over the design and colors. Choosing colors connected me to other worlds—turquoise for the beaches I love but were closed this summer, blue for the skies above the Alps we didn't climb.

Annierose came out to visit in the summer and painted her two planks. Her loyalties have changed from butterflies and ladybugs to cats. She sketched and painted three feline poses. The cats aren't socially distanced from one another but that's okay. For hours at a time, Annierose stood at that table, ignoring the joint pain that juvenile arthritis has inflicted on her since the age of three. I watched her in the garage, focused, relaxed and when maskless, smiling occasionally.

Daniel waited until two days before leaving for college to paint his side, a mirror of the waiting this pandemic has enforced: waiting in a drive-by car line to pick up items from his locker and his cap and gown for pictures at home, waiting for speakers with his masked friends at anti-racism marches, waiting to see if the university campus would open, waiting to move onto campus in the third week of staggered arrivals. He could have painted an unrented prom tux, a lone mortar board thrown into the air, empty recital chairs. Instead he painted what he sees in the future—the dog, any dog, that he's wanted for years.

The rites of passage that would normally enrich the present and map the future vanished. Rational people, which I consider myself to be, are wearing masks but not rose-colored glasses. All we can see is what is in front of us, one brush stroke at a time.

As I paint, I remember the long summer nights around the table with friends, roaring laughter, endless toasts, Sunday morning breakfasts with the five different types of pancakes Uli makes. I can't see the future, but I must believe these gatherings will happen again. I must believe that our country will recover. I must believe that despite the dark challenges of this year, we will have brighter days, weeks, months and years.

I'm painting that tenacity into every swirl. I'm painting glory with every bright color I choose. I'm painting unfettered movement into every design I create. And I'm painting joy and hope for a new future into the sun, a sun that I believe will outshine anything.

BOXED IN

ADRIENNE STEVENSON

it has been eight months now and there is no sign
of letting up our confinement since we have not
found a treatment nor a preventative elixir to
permit even small groups to gather in any form
of social activity like work or play or education
or entertainment and many people are becoming
depressed and angry and just want an end to this
isolation which we are not used to as sociable
apes but the virus is everywhere and we cannot
escape it unless we avoid each other assiduously
and don't succumb to the temptation of
becoming too close so we hover at the ends of
driveways and wear masks in grocery stores and
wash our hands compulsively to ward off an
illness that didn't exist a year ago but is probably
with us forever now and part of our frustration is
the injustice of the disease and the failure of
those we trusted to care for our most vulnerable
ones and treat all groups as decent humans
should be treated so if this is indeed
the apocalypse we will go out with a
whimper not a bang and we will still be boxed in

BARBARA WALTERS, WHY HAVE YOU FORSAKEN US?

JOE QUINN

the murder hornets
followed the storm of plague
the pandemic
the planned depopulation
before "contactless" was a word
when "essential worker" would have smacked
of communist manifesto
sent out from 5G watchtowers
with a message in morse code
"heaven is full,
so sorry"

the pedophiles in hollywood
buying kids in dressers
the race war funded by the soft whites
who send their citizen soldiers off
to die on front lines
to protect and service
the interests of the money hungry minority

this year's calendar hangs like an escaped slave
when it's 9/11 every morning
with an alarm ringing violent white noise

THE ERA OF MEANINGLESS NOISES

KEVIN LAKES

Once we had a fancy thing called rhetoric, but that's gone now. So, depending on who you are, this essay is worthless fluff, or outrage porn, or empty reminiscing. Depending on who you are, if you end up reading it, you could learn something. Or you'll learn something but won't believe it, or you'll refuse to consider whether you've learned anything or not, or you'll debate the concept of learning altogether and join a cult where everyone wears ant colonies as hats. Because, independent of who you are, rhetoric is gone and communication is right behind it.

Facts are relics, opinions are less than worthless, and talking to anyone at all is probably pointless. Our bucket of voices is overflowing.

Nothing means anything.

No one cares.

We live in a post-information society, a reality that's steadily becoming a global phenomenon. So, buckle up, or bail out, since however you respond doesn't matter, because whatever I say is pointless.

Early on in our marriage to neo-authoritarianism, I think some of us retained an ardent hope that the more rational voices would prevail. Now, we're beginning to discover that voices in general are meaningless. In a way, it's fascinating to talk about. But it's framed by the fact that talking about it is useless.

I'm typing out of mere exhaustion, if I'm being honest with myself. Maybe throw in a little quarantine-flavored boredom, for seasoning, and you have a recipe for a literary non-argument about the meaninglessness of information, in an era where meaning has no value.

The notion of traditional rhetoric we used to have was an idea originally traced back, in its official, formal composition, to the Classical Greeks. Aristotle's *On Rhetoric* is undeniably the most

190

recognizable early study of the field today. But there were others, works by the Sophists who proclaimed that rhetoric could be applied to more than just politics and government. You see, said the Sophists, we could also debate the virtues and vices of that last season of *Game of Thrones*, for instance. And if you can find any virtues there then you're a better rhetorician than I am.

In the modern era, rhetoric has been expanded through centuries of work by philosophers and educators, into a formal area of study that barely anyone pays attention to anymore. One ten-minute visit to a freshman composition class will drive this point home. And rhetoric isn't even the only study of discourse in the pantheon of liberal arts. It's simply the most well recognized. There's also linguistics, stylistics, Foucauldian discourse analysis, semiotics, and interdiscursivity, to name a few. Medieval formal education was full of this stuff and its precursors. The Enlightenment and Renaissance thinkers tossed a billion amazing ideas inside a treasure trove of volumes all written in Latin. But no one can read Latin anymore, so don't worry about that.

A lot of this stuff I've never been a fan of and haven't ever formally learned how to use. And that's a problem. It was a problem for my entire generation, and now the newer generations have even *bigger* problems because of it. You see, there aren't many people around anymore who truly know any of this. The closest thing to the genuine use of rhetoric I've seen lately is that list of logical fallacies that circulates on the Internet to teach you how to antagonize people on Facebook. That deeply thorough study aside, it's all been systematically unlearned via a progression of complacency and group think.

The process of unlearning something vital is simple: first, we become convinced that something is so integral to contemporary culture that we've entrenched its modes and philosophies in the minds of every living creature.

Next, we become confident that there's no need to study it anymore because everybody knows it. *We're all good here with this, it's fine.* After a while, people really don't know it anymore, but they recognize that they should. *It's an important keyword! This thing that our parents knew.* We become a tiny bit angry at ourselves, and collectively start to act like we still know it, that it's old hat, and *deep*

191

down we all really understand it intuitively anyway, right? Because you know, it's so vital and stuff.

Of course, before long, we forget about it all together. Because *it's just a thing that old people learned about. It isn't useful anymore.* And maybe that's true of a fair number of topics.

We don't need to know MS-DOS commands or how to navigate by the stars anymore, but when you're talking about the entire field and subfields of interpersonal interaction, then we're going to run ourselves into a whole forest of pickles. And when you combine the most prolific and effective international misinformation campaign ever imagined with the general process of unlearning, organized society never stood a chance.

What we're seeing from our current international cabal of ice cave-dwelling villains is a top-down dismissal of rhetoric and every related field. We are being ruled and governed by people who disregard the fact that interpersonal skills ever existed at all. If you think that doesn't exponentially speed up the process of unlearning, and that the unfortunate (but intentional) target of that unlearning happens to be a skill vital to the adhesion of our species, then I have a bridge full of orange-tinted bronzer to sell you.

In an environment where nothing that's said or written has any value, it's impossible to argue. It's like when you play the game where you repeat a single word until it loses all of its meaning.

I once read a piece on the different forms writing took on during specific eras across time. Satire in response to abuse of power, fantastical leanings in times of scientific enlightenment, escapism in the worst of economic depressions, etc. But something about this particular time mutes every tonal wrapping paper available. Something about it dulls and inebriates even the most focused and diligent rebuttals. I believe that thing to be the sheer scale of the trap we've sprinted into.

I find that most people don't understand just how thorough the undermining of discourse has been. It's possible that the extent of it may never be revealed publicly. Perhaps even the global intelligence communities may not have the full picture. But the state-sponsored misinformation campaigns that have dominated our political cycle for the past decade, and ramped up extensively for the 2016 U.S. Presidential Election, have wreaked havoc on our ability to hold a basic conversation with our neighbor, our friend, our sibling or parent, or even a stranger in line at the grocery store.

Of course, Capitalism isn't content with government-sanctioned shenanigans. Instead, it inspires objectivist copycats of all shapes and forms. And so, we have an epidemic of clickbait slideshows that "prove" a completely benign new study demonstrates the existence of a parallel universe where time runs backward; we have private firms in Macedonia made up of tech-savvy teenagers who thought it would be neat to be rich and found an easy opening; and random suburban dads who run misinformation empires but refuse to comment on their motives when they're finally tracked down. Even if words are meaningless, let's not mince them; this is a nightmare and a genuine existential crisis.

Go ahead and try to argue that science says coastal cities will be underwater in a hundred years. When the less informed have been conditioned to believe that talking points are just as good as facts, and opinions are as esteemed as decades of research, sycophants will still be spouting denials from their rooftops as the flood waters close in around them.

And each new crisis brings more of the same. It isn't happening, and if it is happening, it isn't that bad. Either way, don't pay attention to it, we need to get back to business as usual.

Lead.

Smoking.

Public drinking water.

Endless wars.

Russia.

Climate Change.

COVID-19.

Over and over and over.

The only new development is how efficient the industrial misinformation dispenser has become. The Internet has brought together groups of people in camaraderie who would have previously been dismissed outright and silenced. You could argue that it's a great thing for less-publicized issues that have vastly benefited from more exposure and resources, or you could argue that the net negatives from collecting and empowering sociopathic basement-dwelling keyboard jockeys isn't worth all the Reddit gold in the world. Or you could argue that 5G causes coronavirus. Depending on who you are.

On the Internet and off, this era, let's call it "The Era of Meaningless Noises," expands from multiple directions, not all of them confined to the political right. With the rise of personal "truths," the reliance on factual information has been completely eliminated.

My truth is that the rise of this phrase has become a justification for validating severely misinformed opinions, some of which can be quite dangerous. My truth is that it has poisoned people against facts. It certainly sounds more powerful than having to admit that this truth you speak is actually just how you feel about something, though.

Intersectionality and identity politics, being absolutely necessary and effective tools of equity in a mindlessly white-washed culture, combine with our current atmosphere of *anything goes* with unfortunate results. It isn't the fault of the historically oppressed, who are finding themselves with an audience for the first time, that their voices are merging into the cacophony. It's the fault of the people who don't want to hear them, who are themselves shouting even louder.

We live in a snow globe with poor acoustics, garbled echoes and guttural growls closing in from all degrees of the spectrum.

More often than not, it seems like the most brazen and misinformed voices are the loudest. The flat earthers, the antivaxxers, the X-gaters. I can imagine Bigfoot and the aliens at the edge of the woods watching us wander into even shakier territory, totally devastated and unable to look away. *Hang on, you guys. We're right here.*

In this era of meaningless noises, all of us are totally helpless, whether we recognize it or not. With no shared definitions and no prisoners taken, that old thing called rhetoric couldn't fix things if it tried. In the time it takes to pry open its coffin, someone could knock out a hundred tweets or devour and regurgitate a compilation of YouTube soundbites from the most recent "debate." Was this an intentional weaponization of false equality created by our geopolitical foes, and to some extent, probably ourselves?

Sure, it was.

Was it the unintended consequence of unleashing a flood of perspectives through the most prolific information distribution technology ever available at a time when information itself is under siege?

Absolutely.

Was it rampant anti-intellectualism in response to the continued crises of our mishandled planet, and the economic repercussions of sound, fact-based policy? The deliberate, repeated campaigns by corporate interests to dismiss the consequences of their greed? The rise of gerrymandering and other meddling by power seekers with no sympathy for how the shape of the political landscape would adjudicate the survival of our species?

Yes, yes, and yes. All that and more.

Unfortunately, there's no easy way out of this. In fact, there's probably no way out at all. Our decision makers are old, out of touch, ignorant, greedy. They render decisions on issues they don't understand, ignoring the advice of experts. Those who are acting in good faith or in lip service are repeatedly neutered by the majority who aren't.

We have never before had access to as much information as we do now and yet all of us, collectively, know so very little. In this era, the voices, the echoes, the intellectual regression, all of it reinforces the idea that participating in a society does not require knowledge. And at the moment, that's true, as much as anything is true at all.

We have a complicated journey ahead. But it ends in one of two ways.

We lose—which is the turnout that I find most likely—and make our quiescent toddle into extinction.

Or, less likely, we win. Magically, people stop refusing vaccines because Bill Gates is tracking them with microchips. They read more, they review policy platforms instead of watching debates and treating elections like voting their crush onto homecoming court, we empower workers, we eat the rich.

Or maybe there's a third option to consider here. Maybe we survive the apocalypse to become street-drifting mole people. Although intriguing to think about, this is probably a fantasy relegated solely to fiction. Most of the arguments that people make these days are fiction, so maybe it's not totally off the table after all. Until facts are cool again, extinction or mole people is what we have coming.

Win, lose, mole people, each of these options could prove welcome endings to the story of humanity. Depending on who you are, of course.

ARIEL

JASMINA KUENZLI

For months, I am wrath and sublime.
I am destruction.
Hands and ribcage shake
until my soul comes scrabbling out.
I build up the disasters more and more—
an earthquake, tidal wave, hurricane.
I hurl ships into his coast,
weave his name
into a maelstrom.

But all he does
is take a step backward.
He says, "Come a little closer.
I promise it won't hurt this time."
I know he's lying.
But he says it in the eye of a hurricane,
in the stilted quiet after a storm ends.

My past heartbreaks still linger on the shore,
not quite broken down into silt,
fragments of broken glass
too raw to be spun into sand.
They cut my feet,
and I know the less I fight,
the worse it will hurt.

But he asks me to come again,
so I do.

REASONS TO BELIEVE

CATHRYN MCCARTHY

They curl in my sinews like lice,
sing seaside songs in November mizzle;
time and coal-dust wrinkle the looking glass
while their image remains faithful,

features wiped vacant,
dark hoods plunged forward;
the worm-eyed dreams of medieval monks in plague year,
ruddy apple-cider torsos blooming, fermenting,
poison pipped between yellowed tombstone teeth.

Ice packed in lungs,
I join our Unseelie masque
with hooked breath,
shrink from all love
with petrified tears;
entrails twirling in the dance.
I watch the sagest jackdaws stitch
the pretty blue lips of foundlings.

For she who once hanged in her castellated forest
murmurs *sturm und drang* through our pixelated hammocks—
we all still swing.

BETWEEN CURSED AND CURED

A.M. KELLY

Nothing will ever be less than it is now, Jeremy thought, feeling the cold glide of the egg sliding behind his ear. Grave dirt was clotted in the blood of his split knuckles, but at least he was quick enough to roll away from the kick he saw coming for his kidneys.

I will never be less popular, he thought, pushing himself to his feet and nearly tipping over an old headstone that barely came up to his ankles.

"Get back here you coward-ass son of a whore!" Denny screamed, charging for him. Yes, Denny, like America's favorite casual diner with all-day breakfast. Jeremy was really beginning to question just what in the hell these Indiana parents thought they were doing.

I'll never be less respected, Jeremy reminded himself as he hopped over the headstone that had tripped him.

I'll never be less safe. He scrambled a few feet to a fresh-dug plot, lush with at least 250 dollars worth of flowers. A wreath as big as his chest obscured most of the engraving on the marble. It wasn't much but grabbing it and swinging it full force knocked Denny's hand to the side just in time to save Jeremy from getting a second black eye.

"Hey!" a man's voice boomed, angry authority evident in the tone.

Denny turned to look, a response ingrained in him by years of football coaches and father figures with switches.

Jeremy didn't turn to look, just booked it as fast as he could towards the tan and navy blue Oldsmobile parked by the road. His long legs did him one better than all Denny's decade of practicing tackles. He was twenty feet away before the asshole even moved.

"Denny Owens, don't you turn away from me, Boy!" the groundskeeper screamed. Mr. Rothschild was a good groundskeeper and not a bad guy, from what Jeremy could tell. They met a couple of times before when Jeremy came visiting. Mr. Rothschild didn't take any less care of his mother's grave than any of the others. "You think I don't know that's you? I've known your father since we were both shitting our nappies. You pay attention when I speak."

Jeremy didn't think Mr. Rothschild would come after him now that he had Denny to deal with, but Jeremy wasn't taking any chances. He planted one palm on the hood of the Oldsmobile and flung himself over the hood, Dukes of Hazzard-style.

Holy shit, that actually worked, Jeremy thought, impressed with himself for the first time that week. Half a dozen rabbiting heartbeats later, he was in the driver's seat, slamming the door shut behind him, keys already in hand.

The Oldsmobile always started slowly, with a kick and grumble like an old drunk being told he couldn't sleep at the bar. Still, Jeremy got it into drive and was already peeling away from the cemetery, tires squealing, before the lump of fabric in his passenger seat began to move.

Misty yawned, emerging from her hibernation beneath Jeremy's pea coat as elegantly as the Loch Ness monster rising to take in a bit of the brisk Scottish air. Shoving the now-unwanted pea coat into the footwell only took her a moment, but it was a moment that Jeremy used to run through exactly what he was going to say to explain the mess Denny had made of him.

Unfortunately, as so often happened, his mind was blank.

He could feel her eyes on him. The second she caught sight of the new-forming bruises and mess of egg, a deep nauseating twist of dread wound in his gut.

"How does this keep happening?" Misty said. She threw her arms out to either side of her as she spoke, going from half-asleep to entirely outraged in the span of time it took Jeremy to open his mouth. Her perfectly red lips curled away from her teeth. Professionally arched brows drew in and down, becoming angry slashes over her eyes.

"You know how they feel about mom here," Jeremy said. He was aiming for nonchalance. There wasn't even the slightest chance he hit the mark.

Misty rolled her eyes but bent to dig through the sea of old receipts and crumpled fast food wrappers littering the floor of the Oldsmobile until she came up with some clean-ish takeout napkins. "Well, you're not mom," she said like that was the final word on the subject. "And if they treated mom like this when she was growing up then they got what they deserved."

Jeremy shifted his eyes over to his sister, then slid them quickly back to the road as she began scrubbing at the egg on the back of his head with the wad of napkins.

"I mean, she did curse the whole town, Mist. Like, old school Salem-style seven-generations-of-misery cursed the whole town. It was kind of a big deal."

"Yeah, cursed them with bad soil and tough luck. Puh-lease. They could have paid some little charm-chanting Wiccan to bless them with four-leaf clovers or something. Who even farms anymore? Just get a job at a bank or something for Christ's sakes. What's done is done."

"Pretty sure that's not how the town sees it. Besides, the average charm-chanter would have had to ward every single house individually and bless each person, and probably give them a token to tie it all down, too. It wouldn't stick against a curse that powerful otherwise. That work would take like a year and a half, easy."

"Well, it's been nearly twenty now, so the town can go fuck a duck for all I care," Misty said casually. "They're a bunch of broke-ass hicks with a weird superiority complex. I didn't even want to come here." She punctuated the statement by throwing the eggy wad of napkins in the back seat as hard as she could. "Why did they even have eggs in a cemetery?"

"To desecrate mom's grave," Jeremy said, trying not to feel the sharp bite of anger in his heart as he spoke.

Strong emotions were dangerous for witches. Or, rather, they were dangerous for the people dumb enough to get close to them. There'd been a split second in the graveyard where Jeremy nearly killed Denny. Jeremy had actually felt the throbs of Denny's carotid, how weak those artery walls were, in comparison to a witch's will. By the skin of his teeth, Jeremy managed to wrestle his power back under control.

There was a beat of silence as Misty digested Jeremy's words.

"I know you said no hexing but..." her voice was a lower register than it ought to have been.

Witches, Jeremy thought, *strong emotions. Trapped in a getaway car going 45 in a 30. Through a school zone. Fuck.*

201

"We aren't hexing anyone," Jeremy said firmly. "Grandma was dead serious about cutting us out of the will unless we spend our summers here. It's eggs now but if we escalate things it'll end with them tying us to a stake."

"Well," Misty said, flipping her long platinum blond hair over her shoulder. "I guess it doesn't really matter. Birds shit on those tombstones all day. And it's not like Mom is actually buried there, anyway. All they can do is desecrate the decoy. I'd love to see one of those idiots even step foot in a witches' cemetery."

Jeremy was not stupid enough to listen to what she was saying or the casual tone she was saying it in. He risked looking away from the road just long enough to catch a glimpse of her eyes squinting with feline satisfaction.

"The family grimoire is in Grandma's will," he reminded her. "Priceless artifact of our family's magic. Power beyond anything we could dream of achieving in our lifetimes without it."

"Yes," Misty said, "and at least five hundred thousand dollars each. Enough to set us back up in Vermont without asking Dad for anything. Maybe open up a little herbalism and alchemy shop." Misty's eyes got that far-away longing look that she always wore when thinking about money, cute witch-boys, or Color Pop cosmetics.

"Pretty sure Grandma isn't planning to die for at least another decade, kid," Jeremy said. He felt a little uneasy about the whole conversation, even though he had been the one to bring up the will. He didn't like feeling that they were vultures already picking over her bones while she was still kicking. She might not have been the warmest woman, but she was family and she took good care of them every time they stayed with her.

Misty glared at him. "Don't call me kid when we're the same age, asshole. Don't ever forget that I am three minutes and thirty-three seconds older than you, *little brother.*"

Jeremy let that go, largely because an idea was suddenly barreling through his mind like a mac truck. "Misty. Misty, oh my God."

"Don't tell me you're running out of gas," Misty said. "We're like two blocks from Grandma's."

"Misty, I just had the biggest idea of my life."

"Okay, just hold up a second," she said, grabbing her purse and rooting around inside of it. "Let me see if I can find my magnifying glass."

"Misty," Jeremy said, still breathless with the clarity of this revelation. "What if we break the curse?"

The tires screeched against the pavement as Jeremy pulled sharply onto the long gravel driveway that led to their grandmother's house.

"Break the curse," Misty said slowly. "You want to make life easier for these people? Are you out of your goddamned mind? You've been hit on the head too many times today. I'm making you a poultice and some clarity tea the second we're inside. Don't even think of whining about the smell."

"No, Misty, Mist, listen, this is perfect!" Jeremy's hands flew off the wheel before the car was fully stopped, gesticulating wildly as he tried to get his sister to see how brilliant this plan was.

"Who taught you how to drive?" Misty screamed, as if they hadn't learned together. Her eyes were wide, hands twitching toward the wheel like she only just barely stopped herself from reaching out to grab it. "Christ, Jer! I'm gonna die in this backwater town and it's gonna be your fault."

Jeremy put the car in park.

"We're fine. Listen, if we break the curse, two things will happen: the townspeople won't have a reason to hate us anymore, and the entire witching community will realize how badass we are. Think about what great word of mouth the apothecary will get!"

"Herbalism and alchemy shop," Misty corrected instantly. "You're the one who said mom's curse was some old school Salem shit. How are we even supposed to break that on our own with no grimoire? What about the magical backlash or releasing all that energy? Do you really think all these hicks are gonna roll out the welcome mat even if we do somehow manage it? You never *think*. Grow up, Jeremy."

She was already halfway out of her seat by the time Jeremy said, "They'll fear us."

Misty paused, looking over her shoulder at him. "They'll know we're at least as strong as she was." He continued. "There's two of us and there was only one of her. I know they won't ever love us,

I'm not stupid, but if we can undo the curse, maybe they'll just leave us alone for the rest of the summer."

She sat back in her seat heavily and closed the door.

For a minute there was silence. All Jeremy could do was grip the wheel. *If Misty doesn't agree, there's no way in hell I could do it alone.*

"Fine," she said. "If we can come up with a half- decent plan between the two of us, we'll give it a shot, at least. If it doesn't work we hex them."

"Agreed!" Jeremy said, too happy to even really think about the gamble he was taking on that deal. If the curse had been easy or safe to break it would have been done by now.

Nothing will ever be less than it is now, he reminded himself. There's nowhere to go but up.

* * *

Their Grandma's attic wasn't as dusty as Jeremy remembered, though it did have one of those sit-down hair dryers from 1955 jammed into one corner. The air was heavy, slowly suffocating with its lack of ventilation. It smelled of mothballs with a kick of mint, which was about as unappetizing a combination as Jeremy could think of. Having been built well before residential building safety codes were even a thing, there were certain parts of the attic where he and Misty had to hunch over just to walk through.

"We're gonna fall through a rotted floorboard or something," Misty grumbled, swatting at a cobweb with a rolled up issue of Teen Vogue.

While Jeremy figured out the *how to* of his brilliant plan, Misty sequestered herself in her room for one of her most ancient self-care rituals. She laid out on her bed with a red pen, inking perfect pentagrams next to all the things in the magazine that she wanted. There were a *lot* of bloody stars smeared across those glossy pages.

"Here it is!" Jeremy shouted. The cardboard box he found his mother's old things in had a beige picture of a cookware set on it. From the 1970's if Jeremy guessed.

Inside, a black velvet altar cloth was draped over the cache.

"Okay," Misty said, not sounding happy about it. "So maybe there *are* magical artifacts from Mom's teenage years up here. They're still old as balls though."

Reverently, Jeremy peeled back the black cloth. A puff of dust mushroomed up. Treasure waited below, though, enough to make Misty's sneezing and swearing worth it for Jeremy. Half a dozen crystals in a rainbow of colors, each bigger than Jeremy's palm, all glowing softly with magical energy.

"Whoa," Misty said. Her magazine hit the floor by Jeremy's left shoe. "Motherlode."

"Literally," Jeremy muttered, expecting the whack Misty immediately gave the back of his head, but being unable to resist a good pun anyway.

There were other things in the box too. A worn stack of tarot cards, tied up with a vermillion silk ribbon like a Christmas present. A cord of dark, braided hair bound with what looked like thin strips of leather. Half-burnt beeswax candles, sweetly fragrant even when they weren't on fire, some with bark or herbs or petals poking through the surface of the wax, clearly homemade for magical purposes. A pocket knife with their mother's initials carved into the wood accents on the handle. A mason jar of gleaming glass beads, bent nails, cotton balls, leaves so dark and crumbling they could have been anything, and pieces of a broken mirror.

"When is Grandma gonna be back?" Jeremy asked.

"How should I know?" Misty scoffed.

Jeremy couldn't look away from their haul. He'd seen it once before, that summer after his mom died when he was combing the attic for pictures of her. Proof that she had been there before him (and that she was just as miserable about it as he currently was). That was years ago though, and he was just a kid at the time. Magical artifacts hadn't been nearly as interesting to him as the chance at finding some version of her smile he'd never seen before, captured forever on heavy photo paper.

"Do you think this is what she used to curse the town?" Jeremy said, reaching out to brush his fingers over one of the warm crystals.

"Probably," Misty said. "Why else would she leave it behind when she left?"

Jeremy shrugged.

"We should try it now," Jeremy said. A giddy smile broke across his face.

"*Now?*" Misty said. "We haven't even done any planning! We don't have anything ready."

"Mom got it all ready for us, stupid," Jeremy said. He began unpacking the crystals from the box one at a time. "The crystals will absorb the backlash. They're definitely big enough to store all that. The witch bottle will trap any wayward ill-will." Jeremy held up the mason jar and shook it a little.

"We use the candles to form our circle. This braid of mom's hair will give us a strong enough connection to the spell caster that the breaking itself shouldn't even be *that* hard."

Misty looked down at the box, pursing her lips and arching one eyebrow skeptically.

"I don't know, Jer. This seems even more dangerous and stupid than usual. Why would Mom leave something like this just laying around if it's the key to undoing the spell she made her name on? This all feels a little too convenient. Maybe we should talk to Grandma first, or, I don't know, look through the family library or something."

"Wooooow," Jeremy said, sliding the vowel out for as long as he could hold it. "I never thought you were such a coward, Mist."

"Coward?" she said sweetly, baring her perfectly white teeth. "When this bullshit plan of yours fails, I'll make Mom's curse on this fucking dump look like child's play." Her manicured nails were biting into the flesh of her palms in a way that had to hurt.

"Cool," Jeremy said. "So, you get the salt and charcoal and I'll start setting up the candles and crystals."

"Excuse you," Misty said, biting the words out. "*You* go get the salt and charcoal and *I'll* set up the candles and crystals. Off you go, shoo." She flicked her fingers toward the attic door dismissively.

"You won't regret this, Misty!" Jeremy shouted over his shoulder as he made his way to the attic door, moving as fast as he could while he hunched to avoid hitting his head on the ceiling.

"I already do," Misty said with a sigh.

* * *

The circle they made was a pretty basic thing, though the entwined pattern of charcoal and salt gave it an ass-kicking extra boost of protection. Outside of the circle, the crystals, too, were set up in a ring around them, emitting a quiet, constant light. On the other side of the line, the candles danced merrily, filling the air with a sweet and herbaceous fragrance. Safely tucked in the center of all this were Jeremy and Misty.

Between them the black velvet altar cloth was spread on the ground, which Jeremy had taken outside and shaken thoroughly at his sister's insistence. On top of the altar cloth sat a hand mirror, the pocketknife, and the lock of their mother's hair.

Jeremy took a deep breath, ignoring the tickle against his sinuses from the dusty air. He met his sister's eyes, seeing the seriousness etched there by the shadows and flickering candlelight. Swallowing around his nerves and excitement, Jeremy reached for the braided hair. His sister mirrored him and they each took hold of the leather cords keeping the braid tied together. In unison, they pulled, releasing the knots in the cords and unbinding the hair.

Misty was the first one to reach for the pocketknife. Mournfully, she pulled a lock of her own platinum blond hair out in front of her. The pocketknife sliced through the strands like butter. She handed Jeremy the knife with a frown and began braiding her hair with her mother's.

Though he didn't have much to cut, Jeremy managed to get a few strands of hair from the side of his head without cutting off his ear Van Gough-style. It wasn't nearly long enough to braid but he did the best he could all the same. Once this was done, he knotted one of the leather cords and Misty knotted the other.

They each held a hand over the hair as they closed their eyes. Everything that came before this was kids' stuff. The real challenge would be in the breaking.

Their timing would have to be perfect.

With one voice, they spoke, "We'll call on the curse of Cara Kensington." The hair began to warm up, magical energy flowing between them, through it, collecting and humming with intent.

"We call on the ancient powers, the moon, the sea, the sky, and all the things unseen." The candles flared, hissing and popping.

"We call on the town of Jinsburg and every living thing therein." Jeremy and Misty stretched out their hands without looking, and between their palms the mirror rose, levitating a foot off the ground and spinning like a compass.

"Between binding and breaking, between cursed and cured, we find the path of balance. We walk the gray road. By our breath and by our power, we unwind this curse, now and forever."

They let the mirror drop, shattering with an incongruously loud boom against the floor as they swiftly pulled apart the cords and scattered the hair.

For a second, nothing happened.

They looked at each other. Misty scowled at him, but Jeremy just shrugged.

Then the crystals flared, brighter before blinding white, painful even when the twins covered their faces with their arms.

"What's happening?" Misty screamed.

"Magical backlash," Jeremy said. The dread was already sinking in before the crystals shattered with an ungodly sound like a glacier breaking apart and falling into the sea as nails scraped against a chalkboard.

"Son of a bitch!" Jeremy screamed.

Misty blinked open her eyes. And then blinked a few more times, clearly as blinded as he was by the sudden darkness and the floating spots of light behind his eyes that made him worry about retinal damage.

"Holy shit! Your leg!" Misty said. She pointed a trembling finger at the two-inch chunk of pink quartz sticking out of Jeremy's thigh.

"That shouldn't have been able to get past the circle," Jeremy said. The wound didn't hurt, for which he was grateful even if it was a bad sign.

Misty looked over at the witch's bottle. It was full to overflowing with black, foul-smelling liquid, too thick to be water.

She'd never seen so much resentful spiritual energy collected in one place.

"Do you think it worked?" Jeremy asked, not looking at the chunk of rock lodged in his leg. He would deal with that later. He wasn't sure when, exactly, but later.

"What the hell did you two do!"

"Huh," Jeremy said. "When did Grandma get home?"

Misty was already scrolling through her phone, ignoring her brother.

"Looks like the power is out in the tri-county area," she said, sounding impressed. "We definitely did something."

"Enough of a something to make them fear and respect us?" Jeremy asked hopefully.

"Oh," Misty said. She scrolled more frantically down her feed, her eyes widening as she grimaced. "Oh, shit."

"Misty, just tell me, goddamnit!"

Misty looked up, illuminated only by the blue glow of the phone. "People are saying all the water in their pipes has turned to egg yolk."

"You're fucking with me," Jeremy said.

"I'm not fucking with you," Misty said seriously. "People are posting from all over the county."

"How?" Jeremy said, wild-eyed. He tried to push himself up to stand, only to realize abruptly what a truly awful, terrible idea that was.

"If that hair wasn't Mom's...and we never actually checked the herbs in the candle or the witch bottle...if Mom set this cache up expecting to do another curse...there's so many ways this could have gone wrong. I *did* tell you this would happen, by the way."

"You did *not*!" Jeremy screamed. "You never said that we'd turn the whole county's water supply into fucking egg yolks, Misty. You said we should give it a shot."

"I said we should hex people if it didn't work and that's completely different," she said, flipping her hair over her shoulder. "I'm gonna get Grandma. It might take her a while to make it up the stairs, but she's the only one who can fix this mess now. And your leg." Misty was very pointedly not looking at Jeremy's injury.

209

"Just leave me here to die," Jeremy said, throwing his arm over his eyes, still dancing with phantom lights.

I didn't believe things could get any worse, he thought.

An ominous creak came from the stairs. Jeremy wanted badly to believe that it was just Misty coming back to torment him some more, but in his heart, he knew this was a greater threat. He moved his arm just enough to peek at his grandmother.

She was crouched over to avoid the ceiling beam, her steel-gray hair falling in her face in a way that somehow managed to be both frightening and mysterious. Leaning on her polished oak cane, Grandma stared at him long and hard.

Jeremy avoided her eyes, looking instead at the smooth wood, gleaming proudly in the scant light. A Druid carved it for her long ago, claiming it would be less conspicuous than a staff. The Druid had been right. Even other witches often didn't notice the weapon right away.

"Grandma," Jeremy whined when the silence of her judgmental stare got to be too much for him to bear. "My leg hurts." It was starting to throb, actually. That didn't seem like a positive development.

Grandma sighed.

"You are very much your mother's child," she told him, rubbing her eyes with one long-fingered hand.

That hurt more than the quartz in his leg, even though Jeremy longed to hear those words for years. Tears leaked from the corner of his eyes as the floorboards began to tremble.

"Stop that!" Grandma scolded, stomping her foot once and stilling the magic. "You're too old for those outbursts. What the hell has that useless father of yours been teaching you?" Grandma folded herself down, careful as an origami crane, until she knelt next to Jeremy. She patted his knee, a few inches away from his wound.

Jeremy winced, flinching away.

"Don't be a baby now," Grandma said, gently. "All the good spells come with a little pain. If you can be proud of your finger paintings as a toddler, you can be proud of this mess too. It might have been stupid, but it was powerful. One can often make up for the other. With proper training, you could be an impressive witch one day."

"Oh, no," Jeremy groaned, throwing his other arm over his face as well, like that would stop her next words.

"That's right," Grandma said. "Extra lessons for the both of you, every Friday and Saturday until you leave. I'll make respectable witches out of you yet."

While Jeremy was bemoaning his existence, entirely focused on this very unwelcome news, Grandma yanked out the quartz piece without a word of warning, pressing a wad of gauze over the wound in the same instant.

Jeremy's screams echoed through the cramped attic as Grandma calmly called for Misty to bring up the wound poultice.

Darkness burned at the edges of vision. In the seconds before he passed out, Jeremy reminded himself, *It can always get worse.*

STORMS

N.E. GRIFFIN

Lightning cut across the sky like a web ceaselessly spun and respun by an insane spider. It had been hours since that first black cloud swept over the mountains, since the initial deafening crack of thunder, since the sky tinged greenish-yellow to warn of tornadoes. My beagle, Charlie, trembled under the table in fear during those hours, while I sat on the covered porch watching the lightning create a strobe-light effect across the overgrown acres of my childhood home.

Dad and I used to do this when I was a kid, sit on this porch and watch the summer storms. If he were here, he'd be chain-smoking, refilling his glass of wine, and saying something like, "I've never seen a storm like this in my life!"

So, as proof that we all turn into our parents in the end, that's exactly what I was doing, except I'd updated the cigarettes to an e-cig. "I've never seen a storm like this in my life," I murmured, just to complete the vignette. For whose benefit? Mine, I supposed, for there was no one else left.

I made my way here—zigzagging across the mid-Atlantic on the backest of back-roads, because the I-95 corridor and all the other interstates were clogged with cars, people determined to escape or die trying—in the blind hope that maybe, at the end of the road, I would find my long-estranged father, still alive.

This house, out in the middle of nowhere, was the one place I could think of that maybe the virus had not touched. And even if it had, since I was somehow immune, perhaps Dad was too. All those long miles, a part of me had truly believed I would find him, greyer and balder than I remembered, holding a rifle and threatening to shoot me as a trespasser.

I stumbled up the gravel driveway, holding up my hands and shouting, "Dad!" Nothing but silence greeted me.

I made my way towards the front door, with Charlie following close at my heel, as though something about the place put him on edge.

The house was empty.

There was no sign of Dad, or where he'd gone. His pickup was in the driveway. There was no body or evidence of rushed packing. As far as I could tell, his closet and dresser were full. There was plenty of fishing gear in the basement and guns in the closet. Of course, it had been nearly twenty years since I'd seen him, so I didn't know what his normal arsenal looked like these days.

I gave Charlie a shirt from the laundry, in the hopes that he might pick up Dad's scent and track its owner. When that didn't work, I cursed myself for not properly training Charlie for an emergency like this.

I remembered when I was four, Mom's cat, Petunia, disappeared one day, never to be seen again. At least Petunia had the decency to leave behind a trail of blood in farewell, like a grotesque note saying that she'd gone off to die and not to look for her. Dad had done me no such courtesy.

Of course, he had no reason to expect that I would come to look for him. My mom, brother, and I had all cut him off after he left. If he couldn't take the pressure of Daniel's cancer, fine—we would manage without him. And we did. We survived. Until the next plight to come.

Daniel was hardly the only one to succumb to the virus. Mom too, just a few days later. There were no funerals anymore, the bodies came too fast for that. So, Charlie and I hopped in the car hours after Mom passed and just drove, leaving everything behind.

I shook my head and gulped down more wine. Still too painful to think about that. Easier to think about the numbers, cold and unemotional numbers. It wasn't just my loss, after all. What was the Stalin quote? If one man dies it's a tragedy, if a million die it's a statistic.

Ninety percent of people gone, last radio broadcast I heard. There were no more broadcasts now, at least not official ones. Just static. I had dug an old short-wave radio out of Dad's workbench in the basement and found a few stray stations, broadcasting desperate pleas into emptiness. I switched it off. Better to embrace my isolation than tune in for humanity's death throes.

The world would carry on, I thought, watching the energy course through the sky. All those years of fuss about global warming and now the trees would inherit the Earth. There was some kind of cosmic justice in that, brutally impartial in the way of gods looking down upon humans, as humans upon ants. Perhaps this evening's resplendent sky was some deity's gala celebrating his victory in an ancient wager on the fate of the human race. With fireworks, booming drums, and champagne flowing like a summer downpour.

I figured, may as well join the party, refilling my wine. I watched the electric blue light of my e-cig blaze, its minty vapor pluming into the humid air. I raised my glass.

EMPTY GLASS

HARDARSHAN SINGH VALIA

She ventured into the crowded bar
amidst the invitation to drink and be merry
raised the glass, watched a beading
dissolution of many months of pent-up anxiety
drip down the side and away to the ground.

As the bar closed, begged the bartender
to remove Toulouse-Lautrec's painting,
'Hommage à la Beauté,' hanging
behind the counter because
it reminded her of her grandmother
asking for the last ounce of oxygen.

KEEP SMILING

WM. BRETT HILL

Milo pushed the toe of his worn, leather boot through the charred rubble. It was a risk, returning to his home, and he knew it. Even though the city had been completely destroyed in the first wave of attacks, he knew drone patrols still swept through the area at random intervals. As he scanned the burnt timber and brick, kicking aside discs of melted plastic and shards of glass, he remained conscious of any movement in his periphery.

"Just something. Anything," he whispered as he ran, kicking aside ash and metal. "A reminder of what we had."

His eye caught something different in the landscape of ruin—the corner of a box sticking out from a pile of bricks—and he lowered his rifle and began to dig, finally uncovering, of all things, his mother's recipe box, inexplicably sound amidst the rubble. Eagerly, hungrily, he popped the latch and lifted the lid, his memory flooding with the delicious rosemary and garlic flavor of her pot roast and mashed potatoes. If he could just see some remnant of his family, even his mother's hand-written pumpkin pie recipe, he could find the strength to carry on.

All that sat inside was a letter. He recognized it immediately. His mother had made him write it on New Year's Day, just months before everything went to hell, as he ate his cornbread and collard greens.

"Write a letter from you to you in six months telling yourself what you want from the year. Then in June, we'll open it."

June had come and gone several times since then.

So much had come.

So much more had gone.

Tears ran down his face as he tore open the letter and stared at the words he'd begrudgingly written.

Dear Milo,

Mom is making me write this stupid letter, but she said she wouldn't read it so I can put whatever I want here. I guess she's right. Things do seem promising right now, and it would be good to remind myself of this feeling. I mean, it's cheesy as hell, but it makes sense.

So, to make her happy, here we go:

1. *Mom said if you ace your finals they will buy you a car. I know you did it! I wonder what you're driving...*
2. *If you haven't mustered up the courage to ask Paige Dooley out already, do it tomorrow. If you don't ask, the answer will always be no.*
3. *The future looks bright. It only gets better from here!*

That should be enough to make her happy. Enjoy whatever wonderful thing you are doing (probably cruising around in your awesome ride with your arm around Paige Dooley, you stud!).

And remember, whatever happens, KEEP SMILING!

Sincerely,

Milo

Milo stared at the letter and laughed. "What an idiot I was…" he said, then he looked up. "…am."

The hateful red light on the front of the drone blinked rapidly as the guns slid out of the front of its casing.

He hadn't even heard it descend.

Milo raised his rifle and smiled.

BEFORE IT IS ALL GONE

DAVID HAY

after reading Tristessa
by Jack Kerouac

In manic daydreams of Peter Pan, I dive out
of the hospital window
and catch the birds' notes in my hand
but like water, they overflow my palms
and leak through my fingers;
lost to the silence that is as much
a part of my childhood
as my mother or father.

With my mother dying next to me
in her white nightdress,
with a feeding tube in her nose,
one hand protected by some ridiculous glove thing,
her other hand swollen grotesquely,
nearly matching the glove for size,
it all just makes me feel so sick—
the inevitability of it all,

the emptiness of returning to nothingness.

I write these lines to solidify memory,
to remember what is and not just what was,
to see my mother from all angles and report her truly,
as she was, as she is, snoring into the quiet of the hospital ward,
soon to be gone, dreaming hopefully of her parents,
long absent from this drudgery of day and night;
but I take comfort in her snores and write,
write before all is gone,
before even her snores are lost to the silence.

MY NAME IS ROSA BLANK

ANITA KESTIN

My name is Rosa Blank and I am on my deathbed. By the time you read this, it's likely the brief formalities will be over. The doctor will have filled out the electronic death certificate, listing, I would guess, "Pandemic infection II" as the cause of death. That is what it is called now, for after coronavirus, there was only a short reprieve and then Pandemic II took over and whoever could, ran for cover. I did too, but it got me nonetheless.

I rarely see the doctor now and I take that as a sign that my file has been moved into the hopeless column. Yesterday, I asked my most recent nurse whether I was dying. She pretended not to hear and bustled about with uncommon energy, filling the vases and the water jug, moving the various creams around, and straightening out the bathroom while she ran the water full force for far longer than necessary.

I asked her again as she tried to rush from the bathroom out to the hospital corridor and she told me I was going home. And so, I asked: "Where is that?"

"Home to Jesus," she said and left the room. I doubt Jesus will be expecting me (as I am Jewish), but I have always tried to roll with the punches. In many of the paintings I have seen, Jesus has a kindly face and perhaps Mary will be helping out. Mary often looks like the type of person I might want to get to know but who might be too formal and caught up in her own dramas to become a close friend.

I ponder the nurse's answer and it reminds me of the time that, as a small child, I fell headfirst into a bucket of dirty water and the person cleaning the floor (according to my mother) knelt down and prayed to Jesus to get me out. I never did learn whether Jesus is or is not the type of person who goes around the world pulling babies from dirty water. I tend to think not.

My mother arrived just in time and screamed: "Get the baby out of the bucket!" as she pulled me to safety. When my mother extracted me, it was just one of the many great things she did for me.

I am so tired. My breathing has become more difficult and my respirator priority number is not high enough to ever qualify for a vent. I ring the bell and request some morphine and it comes almost instantly, further confirming that I am on the way out.

* * *

I wake to hear the sound of the trucks outside. There is a letter on my tray table in a double plastic packet which I lack the energy or will to open. There is no possibility of visitors and the charger for my phone no longer works. When this all started, phone calls were a wonderful source of connection but Pandemic II (or "Pan II" as the media tend to call it) has drastically pruned my call list. Even before my charger died, I would call and, with increasing frequency, no one would answer, and eventually I would get a message that the mailbox was full and no further messages could be accepted. Zoom shorted out the internet early on, in case you are wondering about that.

* * *

At the beginning, my family would come to the window and I could wave but I am no longer able to do that on my own and the staff are too busy to help. I am hoping that my family knows that I would if I could, that I didn't suddenly decide that I didn't want to see them. A request: If you can reach my family, can you tell them how much I wanted to see them?

In contrast, I spend hours in my dreams with my parents and their friends, and my teachers, and many of my grade school classmates. I now realize that Sophie was a very nice person, and I may have snubbed her long ago when she offered me half of her sandwich when I forgot mine. There is nothing to be done about that now and I also realize that I can no longer get even at the bully who kicked me with her heavy shoes in fourth grade whenever the teacher went to the bathroom. I go over the names of the teachers in my head and each day I remember fewer of their names. I think I am developing what is

220

charmingly known as "cotton brain." No one would do a CT scan of my head now, but I am very curious as to what it might look like. Would there be patches of nothingness or would all the structures be shriveled? I wonder and fall asleep again.

* * *

The nurse props me up in bed so it must be daytime. She checks my oxygen saturation and I can tell by the expression on her face that it has dropped a bit.

Places I have been dart like eels through my mind, slithery and impossible to hold onto for any length of time. They fuse and merge with seaweed strands and the small purple plants that live by the side of the lake.

* * *

The nurse brushes my teeth and gives me some sort of pill, so it must be night. Dream and dusk tumble over one another like shuffled cards.

I am in the long tunnel up the Jungfrau and there is the ice palace at the top. Here my mother is wandering into the men's bathroom by mistake and being embarrassed as she talks with the man who pointed out her mistake in a friendly way, only heightening her discomfort. My mother's eyes remain firmly fixed on the ceiling as she struggles with the bathroom door, grabs my hand, and pulls me after her into the corridor. Just beyond, there are walls of ice that glow with an orange light.

* * *

I wake and see a mouse scampering across the floor. I call the nurse who says definitively, "there are no mice here." But I can't get over the feeling that there was a mouse and I think about *A Little Princess* where Sara made friends with Melchisedec, the mouse, or was it a rat? Could I make friends with a mouse? I drift and there is the lunch tray.

* * *

There is the Jungfrau tunnel again and I emerge. This time, I see a beach and the swamp beside it with toads and eels and snapping turtles and small fish. Where?

The ground is marshy and makes a sucking sound when I make a step.

The nurse is leading me to the bathroom and the ground consists of linoleum tiles.

* * *

I wake to people standing around my bed and they are shaking me. "You stopped breathing for a while," one of them says. Possibly. I think again about mothers and children and Mary and Jesus and the time my mother was ejected from St. Peter's cathedral because she showed too much skin when she bent to enter the door.

* * *

The room is blue. The splotch on my arm is purple and getting larger.

* * *

People have assembled around my bed. The oximeter is attached to the index finger of my right hand. Now, I think this shaking may be what a seizure feels like from the inside: surprisingly interesting, and not entirely unpleasant. Jungfrau, eels, orange light, Sophie, marshes, Mary-is-she-friend material-or-cold-and-aloof-as-snow?

As I may possibly have said before: by the time you read this, it's likely that the brief formalities will be over.

A POSTCARD FROM THE WISH TOWER

CATHRYN MCCARTHY

I bled my carnal ashes sometime in the 1990s
in a chimney skewed toward the pacific northeast;
they barreled instead toward a faded southern coastline,
a tsunami of smoldering viscera, bone that
vaporized into hysteria and salt-water marijuana,
and so, an elderly couple sat replete on a bench
overlooking a foggy lilac sea.

I learned from this how love endured—
when my oldest window shattered,
the blades pierced shriller than a herring gull's beak.

(You'll have to trust me—I lost my only photograph).

THE DELIBERATE SPEED OF CHAOS

JEFF BURT

It's a deliberate dissembling, picking at edges,
fraying, pulling pieces from the knob of life's bread,
not so much a tornado but an eddy in water
that takes the flotsam and makes it jetsam,
solitude into loneliness, loneliness into depression.

Daily I have thought of us isolated in separate beds
and separate rooms by a ghostly virus, and daily
your loss means this puzzle of life
I have put together loses another piece,
sometimes at an edge, other times in the middle.

Sometimes I wish for a storm that would obliterate
the puzzle completely, but chaos
has a deliberate speed, I can see it ahead
even though part of it has already passed.
Sometimes I wish for the strength to grip
a girder and live through the rending,
but you are my girder, my brace to embrace.

Once I knew the town, the street, the house
in which we lived, knew borders and barriers,
cartography, the discrete villages in which the world
inhabits, physical, mental, spiritual,
yet now is lost, barbed wire clipped
from the fence, space gone formless.

When I woke today, fragrance of your lotion
absent, both the fact and the fantasy,
the immediate sense and the redolence,
missing from the pillow and dresser,
aroma stolen from food, blossom, air,
as if torn away like a riverbank in raging flood-waters.
Not only the ill lose their sense of taste and smell.

I sit slumped in a chair at the end of work, bewildered
by the clock, by the keeping of time,
when time itself was once measured
by the scissoring of our legs, the pulse of your speech,
the monotonous luxury of your sleeping breath.

ASYMMETRIES

PHILIP BERRY

Not all the words they exchange are understood, but that is fine. She is Spanish, trapped in a country she was only supposed to be visiting. He is English, emotions hidden behind strips of iron that were bent around his chest by the heat of tragedy and the rhythmic hammers of recurring grief.

She lies on a raised stone plinth next to the broad steps that sweep down from the Albert Memorial, a gaudy, golden tribute to love, royalty and empire. The sun is strong. It is the tenth summer.

As he stands on a step looking along her horizontal body, distant families and solitary joggers seem to ride over her contours. His gaze moves toward her head, and he notices a scar in the dip at the front of the neck.

One of her hands drops off the plinth. He twitches. She is not to know, but beneath the lip of the plinth is hidden a small metal canister, attached to the stone by a line of glue dots. His son Alec did that. He wanted to leave clues around the city, for the family to find when they returned to the spot. The city is spotted with them. It was Alec's game; but they never had the opportunity to play it.

She moves her head slightly, to adjust the position of the leaves and the branches of the tree that looms over her. She wishes to recreate a particular pattern. She loves the way the edges of the leaves seem to dissolve into the air.

What are you doing? he asks.

She smiles into the sunlight, and her lips move under a wash of green, where chlorophyll filters the strong rays.

Same as you. Remembering moments. Her voice is low, rasping.

He walks up a few steps to shorten the jump up onto the plinth. She allows him to sit next to her. His legs dangle over the side.

226

How many moments can you see from here? he asks. It occurs to him: the things that are familiar here, the tall iron railings, the distant copse, the unused perimeter road, the degraded cycle paths with great cracks in the asphalt that jag along their length, the empty ice cream kiosk with a slipped sign, mean different things to her. Perhaps, if they learn to know each other, they will be able to superimpose their memories and build a common history.

She says, I lay here, just here, nine years ago. Before I met you.

It crosses his mind to lie down next to her, in the place where the other man, the man she must have loved, had lain with her. His nearest hand moves, but a sudden tension rides through her body and her breathing changes. No. Not yet.

It was her idea to come to this plinth. If that lazy hand of hers touches the canister by accident and pulls it free of the glue dots, she will want to open it and inspect the contents. If the little piece of rolled up paper inside is exposed to sunlight, if she reads the message, then it will be destroyed. If he then reveals that Alec, his second child wrote it, their time together here will be altered, stained by personal history. His loss will be front and center, her loss—whatever it is—will be secondary, their new relationship grossly asymmetrical. So, if she finds it he will deny it. He will act: *Oh, what's that you've found? Oh look, a kid's writing, wonder why they left it there?*

People look at them. They see two nervous lovers. One, a man in his fifties. The other, a woman in her thirties. Their imbalance means nothing. Only togetherness matters in this tenth summer.

The hand that wandered near the lip of the plinth rises and settles on her chest. With an index finger, she touches the scar on her neck.

She doesn't talk about it, because it is not remarkable.

She came to England to work in a museum not far from here, hence the density of memories associated with this location. She lived with three friends (though she hardly knew them) in a cramped Earl's Court flat. They were all visitors, but she was the only Spanish one. London was beginning to exert its heavy, drab influence on the strong idealism that had brought her to the city, when the first cases were reported.

227

Then, as the conditions relaxed, they caught it. All four of them. It was no big deal. Then came the second strain, the one that targeted the young. Only she survived, after many weeks in intensive care. The breathing tube changed her voice—there was a dislodging; it bruised her vocal cords.

She guesses his loss quickly.

He carries a weight that she recognized from a distance, and she caught the aura of sadness as she approached the rendezvous point. It is quite obvious to her that this area is bristling with sharp, vivid, echoing memories. She knows he wants to leave.

A man loved her once. A survivor, her age. They met in a hotel, while required to quarantine. When the weather turned, they went cycling together. Hyde Park was a favorite. They would rest there sometimes, breathless, side by side on this plinth. If he, today's he, lies down, his shape will match the outline of the other man. She wouldn't mind if he eased down beside her, though. Perhaps the physical congruence across time would cause a reaction, some kind of spark, or a limited cosmic collapse: the living should not slip into spaces vacated by the dead. It's so hard to love nowadays.

Deep in thought, her physical self relaxes, and she snores. It is her airway, the damage. It makes each breath turbulent; it will never be quite right. He laughs. Her eyes open and she sees his neck arch backwards and his head turn towards her.

Am I *that* interesting?

A big smile spreads over her mouth, the look matching his. She jumps off the plinth and cries, Come on! The Serpentine. There used to be a cafe there. We used to… Her mouth flattens, seals. A rare slip. She cannot allow herself to speak like this. That was another life.

As they walk away, he feigns to adjust a lace, so that he can glimpse the container stuck under the stone lip. It is still there. The little voice that wrote on the slip of paper still circulates in that dark space. He never read Alec's message, and he never will.

CONTRIBUTORS

T.C. Anderson (she/her) is a writer and artist, with work published in literary journals *Capsule Stories, Infinity's Kitchen, The Born at Sea Collective, Zimbell House Publishing* short story anthology *The Dead Game*, and numerous essays for *Emotional Alchemy* magazine. Her forthcoming poetry collection, *The Forest,* will be published with *Riza Press* in November 2020 and will serve as the basis of an art installation being developed with Houston artist Mari Omori. When not writing, Anderson is an award-winning graphic designer in Houston, Texas, currently studying for her BA in Graphic Design & Media Arts from Southern New Hampshire University. You can find more of her poetry work on Instagram @thetcanderson. "The Sad End of a Rainbow" was written June 2020 and "Eat" was written July 2020.

Tina Anton (she/her) has an associate degree in creative writing. Her works have been featured in *Aphelion, Weirdyear, The Rusty Nail, Electric Pulp*, and other publications. You can find her on Twitter at @Dean_Is_Batman. "Lovesick" was written early April 2020.

Philip Berry (he/him) His short fiction has appeared in *Metaphorosis, Headstuff, The Corona Book of SF,* and *Ellipsis Zine.* He also writes poetry and CNF. He is a London-based doctor. "Asymmetries" was written June 2020.

Melissa Boles (she/her) is a writer, storyteller, and impatient optimist from the Pacific Northwest who recently relocated to Tennessee. Her writing focuses on art, mental health, love, and the human connection. Melissa has been published in *The Daily Drunk, Emerge Literary Journal, Stone of Madness Press*, and at *Fanfare and Sexology* on Medium. Her debut chapbook, *We Love in Small Places,* will be released via *ELJ Publications* in May 2021. You can find her at MelissaBoles.org or at @mmelloftheball. "Lukewarm Cake" was written Spring 2020.

J.S. Bowers (he/him) is a fiction writer, novelist, and editor of *Nobody's Wife,* the memoirs of Joan Haverty Kerouac. "The Elves and the Shoe Designer" was written September 2020.

Beth Boylan (she/her) now lives and teaches high school English near the ocean in New Jersey, though originally from New York. Her poems have appeared in journals such as *Glass, Jelly Bucket, Chronogram*, and *Oyster River*. "Power Outage" was written August 2020 during an actual power outage.

Marianne Brems (she/her) is a long-time writer of trade books, textbooks, and poetry. She has an MA in Creative Writing from San Francisco State University. *Finishing Line Press* will release her chapbook *Sliver of Change in 2020*. Her poems have appeared in literary journals including *The Pangolin Review, La Scrittrice, The Sunlight Press, Armarolla, Foliate Oak*, and *The Tiny Seed Literary Journal*. She lives in Northern California. "Uninvited" was written September 2020.

David Brookes (he/him) is a writer currently living in the UK, from where he runs his editing firm The STP Literary Service. He has stories published in many magazines including *Scrittura Magazine, Every Day Fiction, Electric Spec, Pantechnicon, Bewildering Stories, Whispering Spirits, Morpheus Tales, The Cynic,* and *Aphelion*. His fiction has appeared in printed anthologies, most recently *Aloe*, a collection of stories written during lockdown. His first novel, *Half Discovered Wings*, was published internationally by *Libros International* in 2009. Read more about his work at stpediting.wordpress.com. "The Destination Before Next" was written Spring 2020.

Jeff Burt (he/him) lives in the Central Coast of California. He works in mental health, and has contributed to *Tar River Poetry, Williwaw Journal, Willows Wept*, and *Heartwood*. "The Deliberate Speed of Chaos" was written July 13, 2020.

Megan Cannella (she/her) is a Midwestern transplant currently living in Nevada. For over a decade, Megan has bounced between working at a call center, grad school, and teaching. She has work in or forthcoming from @PorcupineLit, @dailydrunkmag, @VerseZine, @TBQuarterly, and @perhappened. Her social handle is @megancannella). "Migration" was written August 2020.

Dot Dannenberg (she/her) lives outside of Washington, DC. She holds an MFA from Pacific University. One of these days she's going to get her act together. "We Are Living" was written July 11, 2020.

Daphne Daugherty (she/her) graduated from Missouri State University with an MA in Writing in 2014 and currently lives in Eau Claire, Wisconsin, while pursuing a Ph.D. in English at the University of Wisconsin-Milwaukee. She is the author of *Rock N Soul*, a novel published by *Riptide Publishing*, and has only recently begun finding homes for her poetry. "untitled (these walls almost contain you)" was written July 15, 2020. "Recipe For Wild Rice" was started July 19, 2020 and completed September 9, 2020. "Meditation on the Heat Death of the Universe" was written October 6, 2020.

Pam R. Johnson Davis (she/her) is a writer, poet, singer, and educator residing in Chicago, IL. She loves writing poetry, especially as she navigates life, loss, and love. Her first book, *Seasons (I'll Be Seeing You): A collection of poems about heartbreak, healing, and redemption* debuted at the #1 spot for New Releases in African-American Poetry and Women's Poetry on Amazon and won the "Best Urban Poetry" Book Award at American Book Fest in August 2020. "5 a.m. Conversations with a Friend" was written October 7, 2020.

Grace Alice Evans (she/her) is a LGBTQ+, mixed-heritage poet, writer, sound/visual artist, survivor, and a witch. Her work explores living with mental illness, trauma, recovery, and the dichotomy between the inner and outer worlds. Grace's social media handle is @graccaliceevans. "particles" was written Summer 2020.

Louis Faber (he/him). Lou's work has previously appeared in *Atlanta Review, The Poet (UK), Dreich (Scotland), The Alchemy Spoon (UK), Arena Magazine (Australia) Exquisite Corpse, Rattle, Eureka Literary Magazine, Borderlands: the Texas Poetry Review, Midnight Mind, Pearl, Midstream, European Judaism, Greens Magazine, Afterthoughts, The South Carolina Review,* and *Worcester Review,* among many others, and has been nominated for a Pushcart Prize. A novel remains, forlornly, looking for a home. "In Chorus" was written April 18, 2020 and "A Hasty Burial" was written October 19, 2020.

Helen Faller (she/her) is a single-mother anthropologist with a PhD from the University of Michigan. Her work-in-progress, *Love Feasts: A Memoir of Dumplings—and Divorce—On the Silk Road* (83,000 words), tells the story of how she ran away from her divorce in Philadelphia to the Silk Road to learn how to make dumplings and mend her broken heart. She posts about dumplings to some 10,000 followers at mosaiqa.com and social media outlets. She lives in Berlin with her eleven-year-old daughter. "Return of Innocence" was written Spring 2020.

Dónal Forgarty (he/him). Dónal's fictional and factual works span a variety of genres. He teaches academic communication at colleges on both sides of the

Atlantic. His irreverent spoken word poetry on a theme of education has been performed at the University of Nottingham and Exeter College, Oxford. He has also written and edited scripts for the UK stage and radio. He is currently seeking representation. "Tomorrow, James, and the Blue Cat" was written between April and May 2020.

Rachel A.G. Gilman (she/her) has been published in journals throughout the US, UK, and Australia. She is the Creator/EIC of *The Rational Creature* and was EIC for *Columbia Journal*, Issue 58. She holds an MFA in Writing from Columbia University and is currently reading for an MSt in Creative Writing from the University of Oxford. "The Rabbit, The Owl, and The Newt" was written April 2020.

Robin Gow (they/them) is a trans and queer poet and young adult author from rural Pennsylvania. They are the author of *Our Lady of Perpetual Degeneracy* (*Tolsun Books* 2020) and the chapbook *Honeysuckle* (*Finishing Line Press* 2019). Their first young adult novel comes out in 2022. "On Queerness and Dogs" was written September 25, 2020.

Shannon Frost Greenstein (she/her) resides in Philadelphia with her children, soulmate, and cats. She is the author of *Pray for Us Sinners*, a collection of fiction from *Alien Buddha Press*, and *More*, a poetry collection by *Wild Pressed Books*. Shannon is a Pushcart Prize and Best of the Net nominee, a Contributing Editor for *Barren Magazine*, and a former Ph.D. candidate in Continental Philosophy. Her work has appeared, or is forthcoming, in *McSweeney's Internet Tendency, Pithead Chapel, X-R-A-Y Lit Mag, Cabinet of Heed, Rathalla Review*, and elsewhere. Follow Shannon at shannonfrostgreenstein.com or on Twitter at @ShannonFrostGre. "Faith" was started October 10, 2020 and completed November 26, 2020.

John Grey (he/him) is an Australian poet, US resident, recently published in Soundings East, Dalhousie Review and Connecticut River Review. His latest book, "Leaves On Pages" is available through Amazon. "First Touch" was written September 2020.

N. E. Griffin (she/her) lives in Arlington, VA and works for the federal government. She is a lifelong writer who dabbles in fiction, poetry, and occasionally creative non-fiction. Her work recently appeared in the *Constellate Literary Journal, the Poetry and Covid project*, and the *Dear Leader Tales* anthology by *Feral Cat Publishers*. You can follow her on Instagram and Twitter @n_e_griffin. "Storms" was written July 2020.

SK Grout (she/they) grew up in Aotearoa/New Zealand, has lived in Germany and now splits her time as best she can between London and Auckland. She is the author of the micro chapbook *to be female is to be interrogated* (2018, *the poetry annals*). She holds a post-graduate degree in creative writing from City, University of London and is a Feedback Editor for *Tinderbox Poetry*. Her work also appears in *Cordite Poetry Review, trampset, Banshee Lit, Parentheses Journal, Barren Magazine,* and elsewhere. More information can be found at skgroutpoetry.wixsite.com/poetry. "In Retrograde" was written Spring 2020.

David Hay (he/him) is an English Teacher in the Northwest of England. He has written poetry and prose since the age of 18 when he discovered Virginia Woolf's *The Waves* and the poetry of John Keats. These and other artists encouraged him to seek his own poetic voice. He has currently been accepted for publication in *Dreich, Abridged, Acumen, The Honest Ulsterman, The Dawntreader, Versification, The Babel Tower Notice Board, The Stone of Madness Press, The Fortnightly Review, Nine Muses Poetry, Green Ink Poetry, Dodging the Rain, The Morning Star* as well as *The New River Press 2020 Anthology*. "Before it is all gone" was written Spring 2020.

Lindsey Heatherly (she/her) is a writer born and raised in Upstate South Carolina. She has words in or forthcoming with *Pithead Chapel, X-R-A-Y, Emrys Journal, Schuylkill Valley Journal,* and more. She spends her time at home raising a strong, confident daughter. Find her online at r3dwillow.wixsite.com/rydanmardsey or on Twitter @rydanmardsey. "roots of our marrow" was written October 10, 2020.

Wm. Brett Hill (he/him) grew up outside Athens, Georgia but now makes his home on the Eastern Shore of Maryland where he spends time with his wife and daughter, works in IT, and writes stories. His short fiction has appeared in *Literally Stories, Fireworks, Dime Show Review, Flash Fiction Magazine, Digging Through the Fat,* and many more. "Keep Smiling" was written October 17, 2020.

Claire HM (she/her) teaches English and literacy to migrant communities in Birmingham, UK. She's recently had poetry published in *Black Flowers, streetcake,* and on *Mooky Chick*. In October 2021, her debut novella *How to Bring Him Back* will be published by *Fly on the Wall Press*. "slowly then all at once" was written April 2020.

Olaitan Humble (he/him) is a poet and feature writer. A Pushcart Prize Nominee. He is an aviphile and pacifist who derives pleasure from collecting quotations and astrophotos. He won the People's Choice Award in Earnest

Writes Poetry Prize Awards, 2020. He is a Poetry Reader for *Bandit Fiction*, and Poetry Editor for *The Lumiere Review*. His work appears in *The African Writers Review, Luna Luna Magazine, CP Quarterly,* and *Doubleback Review*, among others. Instagram/Twitter: @olaitanhumble. "Benzodiazepines" was written August 2020.

Meagan Johanson (she/her) writes from her lair in Oregon. She has been published in *Berkeley Fiction Review, Emerge Literary Journal, Lunate Fiction*, and elsewhere. She loves music, books, new obsessions, and anything with butter on it. You can find her on Twitter @MeaganJohanson. "Migration" was written July 2020.

A.M. Kelly (she/her) is an author of fiction and poetry. Her short story "Cracked Brown Tile" won the Scribblers Literary Prize in 2015 while her shorty story "Blackberries" received an honorable mention for the same in 2016. She is a member of the Buffalo Writers' Meetup, where she takes great joy in meeting and workshopping with other writers. In her free time, A.M. Kelly is a prolific baker with a deep appreciation for French patisserie in particular. "Between Cursed and Cured" was written Fall 2020.

Anita Kestin (she/her), M.D., M.P.H., is a physician who has worked in academics, nursing homes, hospices, public health, and the locked ward of a psychiatric facility. She is also the daughter (of immigrants fleeing the Holocaust), a wife, a mother, a grandmother, and a progressive activist. Although she has been writing for many years, she has only started to submit work (fiction, nonfiction, and poetry) during the pandemic. Her first non-scientific piece was accepted when she was 64 years old. "My Name is Rosa Blank" was written July 2020.

Kayla King (she/her) is the author of *These Are the Women We Write About*, a micro-collection of poetry published by *The Poetry Annals*. She is the founder and Editor-in-Chief of *Pages Penned in Pandemic: A Collective*. Kayla's fiction and poetry has been published by *Firewords Magazine, Sobotka Literary Magazine,* and *Capsule Stories*, among others. You can follow Kayla's writing journey at kaylakingbooks.com or her twitterings @KaylaMKing. Kayla wrote one poem every day in the month of April to celebrate National Poetry Month. As such,"How to Write Accidents" was written April 2, 2020, "Things to Leave on the Mantle, or Lies We Tell the Dark" was written April 3, 2020, "Only" was written April 10, 2020, and "Real People Who Once Lived in Old Houses" was written April 11, 2020.

Jason de Koff (he/him) is an associate professor of agronomy and soil science at Tennessee State University. He lives in Nashville, TN with his wife, Jaclyn, and his two daughters, Tegan and Maizie. He has published in a number of scientific journals and has over 30 poems published or forthcoming in literary journals this year. "Navigating New Worlds" was written August 15, 2020.

Margaret Koger (she/her) is a Lascaux Prize finalist. She's a school media specialist with a writing habit who lives near the river in Boise, Idaho and writes to add new connections to the wayward web of life. See poems on: *Amsterdam Quarterly, Thimble, Trouvaille Review, Tiny Seed Literary Journal, Ponder Savant, Subjectiv*, and *Last Leaf*. "The Way" was written November 2020.

Jasmina Kuenzli (she/her) is an author of poetry, creative nonfiction, and fiction. When she isn't writing, Jasmina can be found weightlifting, running, and holding impromptu dance parties in her car at traffic lights. Her life goals include landing a back flip, getting legally adopted by Dwayne "The Rock" Johnson, and being a contributor on "Drunk History." She would like to thank Brenna and Sarah, who hear all these stories first, and Harry Styles, who is sunshine distilled in a human being. "Ariel" and "The Sea Witch" were written August 2020.

John Lambremont, Sr. (he/him) is an award-winning poet from Baton Rouge, Louisiana, U.S.A., where he lives with his wife and their little dog. John holds a B.A. in Creative Writing and a J.D. from Louisiana State University. He is the former editor of *Big River Poetry Review*, and has been nominated for The Pushcart Prize. John's poems have been published internationally in many reviews and anthologies, including *Pacific Review, Clarion, The Minetta Review, Sugar House Review*, and *The Louisiana Review*. John's full-length poetry collections include *Dispelling The Indigo Dream* (*Local Gems Poetry Press* 2013), *The Moment Of Capture* (*Lit Fest Press* 2017), *Old Blues, New Blues* (*Pski's Porch Publishing* 2018), and *The Book Of Acrostics* (*Truth Serum Press* 2018). His chapbook, *What It Means To Be A Man (And Other Poems Of Life And Death)*, published in 2014 by *Finishing Line Press*. John enjoys music, playing his guitars, fishing, and old movies. "Haiku in Lockdown" was written May 2020.

Kevin Lankes (he/him) holds an MFA from Sarah Lawrence College. His fiction and nonfiction have appeared in *Here Comes Everyone, Pigeon Pages, Owl Hollow Press, The Huffington Post, The Riverdale Press*, and countless blogs, webpages, and other media. His short story "She Turns the Final Page" was nominated for Best Small Fictions 2019. In his lifetime, he has survived cancer, toured the U.S. in a minivan, and played lead trumpet in a professional polka band. You can find more of his work at kevinlankes.com or follow him on Twitter at @KevinLankes. "The Era of Meaningless Noises" was written Spring 2020.

Jasmin Lankford (she/her). Jasmin's debut poetry collection, *Don't Forget to Water the Flowers*, is forthcoming from *Vital Narrative Press*. Her work has been published in several journals including *Kissing Dynamite, Parentheses Journal*, and elsewhere. Learn more at jasminlankford.com. "Ocean and Orca" was written August 2020.

Lucia Larsen (she/her) is currently studying for her MSc in Environmental Management at the University of Stirling. Her recent work has appeared in *Tealight Press, Neuro Logical, Tipping the Scales*, and *Fever Dream*. She can be found on Twitter @mslucialarsen. "Spell" and "Heart" were written September 2020.

Anthony Leiner (he/him) is a Hudson Valley local that graduated from SUNY New Paltz in 2015 with a BA in Theatre and Creative Writing. After beginning his career in acting, Anthony soon realized he was more at home creating stories than playing in them. Some of his works include: "On the Floor," "Our Cuckoo Bird," and "Hearts and Minds." His plays have been produced by the *Rosendale Theatre, Urban Stages Theatre Company,* and *The Manhattan Repertoire Theatre*. Some of his biggest achievements include winning first place in the Manhattan Rep. 2017 Winter Short Play Contest and directing/ producing Moments: A short play festival at the Morton Library (A short play festival consisting of five of his original works). Along with play writing, Anthony has directed plays other than his own. Most notably, a found space production of "Dog Sees God" by Bert V. Royal, produced by *Paper Rain Productions*. "The Drive Home" was written September 2020.

Justin Maher (he/him) is a writer currently residing in Brooklyn, NY. With poetry making up the majority of his works, Justin experiments with other forms whenever creative inspiration strikes. He graduated from SUNY Brockport and holds a BS in Marketing with a minor English. If asked what his true degree is in, however, he would say wanderlust remains an unending study; for the world is not small and he wants to see and sniff it all. It has been said that travel makes him salivate. Justin is the co-founder and co-editor of *Pages Penned in Pandemic: A Collective*. "52, or, I'm going to blame this on martinis" was written April 2020. "The Bridge" was written mostly in June 2020 and completed in December. "Frayed" and "There are some crows..." were both written early May 2020 before being finalized December 2020.

Meghan B. Malachi (she/her) is a data analyst and poet from the Bronx, NY. Her work is published or forthcoming in *Milly Magazine, NECTAR Poetry, Hispanecdotes, giallo lit*, and *Writers With Attitude*. Her first chapbook, *The Autodidact*, is forthcoming in December 2020. She lives in Chicago, Illinois. "Sour" and "21 Years" were written October 2020.

Emily Manthei (she/her) is an American filmmaker and journalist based in Berlin. Her work focuses on culture, migration and subculture, from a real-world, humorous lens. It has appeared in publications like *Huffington Post, Daily Beast, Deutsche Welle and Open Skies*, among other publications. She's made short films in North and Central America, Europe and Asia, which have appeared in (and won) film festivals all over the world. "Männer LOL" was written August 2020.

Jenny Maveety (she/her) is a third grade teacher and mother to a fiercely independent and bright 6 year old. She has been telling stories since before she could read and has written poetry, short stories, and a novel over the last several years. Jenny is currently working through SNHU's MFA program in fiction writing. Some of her favorite authors include Ray Bradbury, Margaret Atwood, and Anthony Doerr. "Transition" was written early April 2020.

Cathryn McCarthy (she/her) has adored words all her life, writes queer romantic fiction, and has recently developed an all-consuming crush on poetry. Her inspiration ranges from inner city life and grotty jobs to rural landscapes and their ancient folklores (occasionally jumbling them all together.) Publications include *Acid Bath Publishing's Wage Slave* anthology, *Odd Magazine* (September 2020), *Floodlight Editions* (October 27 2020), *Pens of the Earth* (November 2020) and *Versification* (January 2021). She holds a PhD in Cultural History from University College London. "A Post Card From the Wish Tower" was written August 7, 2020 and "Reasons to Believe" was written October 2020.

Carol McGill (she/her) has had work appear in *Capsule Stories, Sonder, Crannóg, Q/A Poetry, Silver Apples Magazine, Brilliant Flash Fiction*, and the anthology *Words To Tie To Bricks*. She founded the Morning Coffee Writing Competition with *Sonder Magazine*. She was the 2019-2020 chairperson of Trinity Literary Society. She tweets at @WordsByCarolx. "No proper burial" was written August 2020.

Corey Miller (he/him) was a finalist for the F(r)iction Flash Fiction Contest (Spring '20) and shortlisted for The Forge Flash Competition ('20). His writing has appeared in *Third Point Press, Pithead Chapel, Lost Balloon, Hobart*, and elsewhere. When not working or writing, Corey likes to take the dogs for adventures. Follow him on Twitter @IronBrewer or at coreymillerwrites.com. "The Distance is Harrowing. The Temperature is Miles." was written Summer 2020.

Matthew Miller (he/him) teaches social studies, swings tennis rackets, and writes poetry - all hoping to create home. He and his wife live beside a dilapidating orchard in Indiana, where he tries to shape dead trees into playhouses for his four boys. His poetry has been featured in *River Mouth Review, Club Plum Journal,* and *Ekstasis Magazine.* "To-Do Lists" was written April 27, 2020.

James Morena (he/him) learned his MFA in Fiction at Mountain View Grand in Southern New Hampshire. His stories have been published in *Amoskeag Journal, Forge Journal, Rio Grande Review,* and others. He also has published essays and poems. James teaches English at university and high school levels. "Evidence of Annihilation" was written July 2020.

Ben Nardolilli (he/him) currently lives in New York City. His work has appeared in *Perigee Magazine, Red Fez, Danse Macabre, The 22 Magazine, Quail Bell Magazine, Elimae, The Northampton Review, Local Train Magazine, The Minetta Review*, and *Yes Poetry*. He blogs at mirrorsponge.blogspot.com and is trying to publish his novels. "Zoonotic" was written Winter 2020.

Christy Nolan (she/her) is no stranger to reflecting on the uncomfortable with meter and alliteration and has always found comfort in the notes of her hand-me-down, cracked-up iPhone. The isolation brought on by the pandemic extended Christy the space to find purpose, confront the past, and rediscover parts of herself she'd forgotten she loved. Christy lives a wonderfully middle-class life in Buffalo, NY and fell in love with the ordinary before she knew what that meant. Laughing or crying, she's grateful for any opportunity to feel; she hopes her work encourages the same in you. "For Body, For Mind" was written Summer 2020.

Wim Owe (he/him) was wearing masks before it was mandated. He's a WA-BC cross border baby living in Victoria and missing his Seattle friends and relatives. "[untitled]" was written midnight between June 5th-June 6th 2020 beneath a full moon.

James Penha (he/him). A native New Yorker, James has lived for the past quarter-century in Indonesia. Nominated for Pushcart Prizes in fiction and poetry, his work has lately appeared in several anthologies: *The Impossible Beast: Queer Erotic Poems* (Damaged Goods Press), *The View From Olympia* (Half Moon Books, UK), *Queers Who Don't Quit* (Queer Pack, EU), *What We Talk About It When We Talk About It*, (Darkhouse Books), *Headcase*, (Oxford UP*)*, *Lovejets* (Squares and Rebels), and *What Remains* (Gelles-Cole). His essays have appeared in *The New York Daily News* and *The New York Times*. Penha edits *The New Verse News*, an online journal of current-events poetry. Twitter: @JamesPenha. "In Due Course" was written November 2020.

Joe Quinn (he/him) is a poet from Kentucky. His newest collection, *We Are Plague* is now available for purchase. "barbara walters, why have you forsaken us?" was written November 2020, just before the election.

Elizabeth Reed (she/her) is an author, musician, political activist and traveler. Her essays have been published in *The Rumpus, Entropy, Mothers Always Write*, and other journals. "The Picnic Table" was written September 2020.

Susan Chock Salgy (she/her) studied creative writing at Brigham Young University, and writes poetry, essays, and non-fiction. Recent publications include her essay, "Indelible", which appears in *Glassworks Magazine*, and poetry appearing in *The Sunlight Press* and *The Magnolia Review*. "The COVID Interregnum" was written between May-June 2020.

Ash Slade (she/her) lives in CT. She has written poetry for fifteen years starting at 13. In her spare time, Ash enjoys reading poetry, studying the Bible, and spending time with loved ones. Previous publications include *The Blue Nib* and *Circus of Indie Artists: Nevermore Edition* edited by Dale Bruning. "On This Road We Go Down" was written October 2020.

Preston Smith (he/him) is an MA candidate in literature at Wright State University. He is a poetry editor for Periwinkle Literary Journal, and his debut chapbook, *Red Rover, Red Lover*, released from *Roaring Junior Press* in early 2020. He can be found on Twitter (and Instagram!) @psm_writes tweeting about his cats, baking, and fairy tales. His poems appear in *Black Bough Poetry, Nightingale & Sparrow*, and *Pink Plastic House*, among others. "To the Boy in California" was written July 2020 and "Rebuilding Wonderland" was written August 2020.

Mitchell Solomon (he/him) studied Writing, Marketing, and Economics at Washington University in St. Louis, where he earned his B.S. in 2011. Since then he has been working in marketing in San Francisco and writing poetry and short stories. "Birdsong" was written Fall 2020.

Tracy Rose Stamper (she/her) dances with words. Her recently acquired middle name is the most significant word she has written lately during these days asking us to rise. She lives in a home on a hill in St. Louis with two beloved humans, two rescue beagle boys, and two whimsical wind sculptures. She is a columnist at *Rebelle Society*, contributing author of Anna Linder's '*The Book of Emotions*,' and has had work appear in *Drunk Monkeys, New Feathers Anthology, Dime Show Review, Feels*, and *Six Sentences*, among others. You can find her dancing with words at facebook.com/DancingPenTracyStamper. "Stone Silver Bird Blessings" was written Spring 2020.

Adrienne Stevenson (she/her) is a retired forensic scientist living in Ottawa, Ontario. Her poetry has been published in *Constellate Literary Journal, Still Point Arts Quarterly, Bywords, Quills, Scarlet Leaf Review, Blood & Bourbon, The Wire's Dream, The Literary Nest, The Poet-On the Road*, and several chapbook anthologies. "Boxed In" was written between July-November 2020.

Stephanie Kadel Taras (she/her) has authored multiple books in twenty years as a freelance writer in Ann Arbor, Michigan, including the award-winning college history *On Solid Rock* and memoir *Mountain Girls*. Her work has also been published in *Bear River Review, Yellow Arrow Journal, Belle Journal*, and the *Ann Arbor Observer*. "Summer Solstice Inside" was written June 2020, just after the summer solstice.

Junpei Tarashi (he/it) works as an Editor to the *Agapanthus Collective* and thinks often about how much of a better life frogs lead. Their most recent work has appeared in *Chambers, The Open Culture Collective,* and *After Happy Hour Review*. "Thanatos Tales" was written August 28, 2020 and "Beast Beats" was written September 19, 2020.

Caroline Taylor (she/her). Ms. Taylor's short stories have appeared in several online and print magazines. She is the author of five mysteries and one short-story collection. "Indispensable" was written April 2020.

Jerica Taylor (she/they) is a non-binary neurodivergent queer cook, birder, and chicken herder. Their work has appeared in *Schuylkill Valley Journal, Postscript, Stone of Madness, and perhappened*. She lives with her wife and young daughter in Western Massachusetts. Twitter @jericatruly. "For the

240

Hopeless Scroll Under the Swipe of Your Finger" was written at the end of October 2020, heading into the week of the US election.

Sher Ting (she/her) has lived in a land of eternal summer, otherwise known as Singapore, for 19 years before spending the next 5 years in medical school in Australia. She has been published in *Trouvaille Review* and has work forthcoming in *Eunoia Review* and *Door Is A Jar Literary Magazine*, among others. She is currently an editor of a creative arts-sharing space, known as *INLY Arts*. "Day 49" was written April 2020.

Brittney Uecker (she/her) is a youth librarian and writer living in rural Montana. Her work has been published by *Waste Division* and *Stone of Madness Press* and is forthcoming for *Second Chance Lit*. She is @bonesandbeer on Twitter and Instagram. "Lance" was written Spring 2020.

Hardarshan Singh Valia (he/him) is an Earth Scientist. Besides contributing mostly to scientific journals, he has published poems, stories, and essays in journals such as *Wards Literary Journal, Northwest Indiana Literary Journal, Poetic Medicine, River babble, Who Writes Short Shorts, Dove Tales – Writing for Peace- an anthology, Dreamscapes – an anthology, Caesura, Sage-ing, Literary Veganism, COVID tales journal, Huffington Post, Northwest Indiana Times*, and in books such as *Diamonds-75 Years of Indiana Poetry, Hoosier Horizon, A Magic Hour Family Christmas*, and *Undeniably Indiana* (Indiana University Press). "Empty Glass" was written July 4, 2020.

Lisa Lerma Weber (she/her) is a writer living in San Diego, CA. Her words and photography have been published online and in print. She is a junior editor for *Versification*. "Fallen Nest" was written Summer 2020.

ABOUT THE COLLECTIVE

Pages Penned in Pandemic: A Collective celebrates the work created during tough times. We believe sharing stories remains our greatest magic and strength in staying connected. Here's hoping you do, too.

All proceeds from the print collective will be donated to *826 National*, an organization which benefits young writers aged 6-18.

To learn more, visit the collective page at kaylakingbooks.com or follow us on Twitter @PagesPandemic and Instagram @pagespennedinpandemic.

Made in the USA
Coppell, TX
21 January 2021